One-Income Household

How to Do a Lot with a Little

SUSAN REYNOLDS WITH LAUREN BAKKEN, CPA

BUSINESS

Avon, Massachusetts

We dedicate this book to all the families who struggle to live on one income in today's world. As two single mothers who raised children on their own for many years, we know the obstacles one-income families face, and we have both empathy for those who struggle and admiration for those who navigate the waters successfully. Yes, you can live on one income!

Published by Adams Business,
an imprint of Adams Media, a division of F+W Media, Inc.
57 Littlefield Street, Avon, MA 02322. U.S.A.
www.adamsmedia.com

ISBN 10: 1-60550-133-6
ISBN 13: 978-1-60550-133-8

Printed in the United States of America.

J I H G F E D C B A

Library of Congress Cataloging-in-Publication Data
is available from the publisher.

This publication is designed to provide accurate and authoritative information with regard to the subject matter covered. It is sold with the understanding that the publisher is not engaged in rendering legal, accounting, or other professional advice. If legal advice or other expert assistance is required, the services of a competent professional person should be sought.
—From a *Declaration of Principles* jointly adopted by a Committee of the American Bar Association and a Committee of Publishers and Associations

Many of the designations used by manufacturers and sellers to distinguish their product are claimed as trademarks. Where those designations appear in this book and Adams Media was aware of a trademark claim, the designations have been printed with initial capital letters.

This book is available at quantity discounts for bulk purchases.
For information, please call 1-800-289-0963.

Contents

Acknowledgments

We would like to thank Paula Munier, director of innovation and acquisitions; Chelsea King, our enthusiastic editor; Katie Corcoran Lytle, project manager; and everyone at Adams Media who helped this book come to fruition. Adams Media is a company that prides itself on providing books that delve deeply into complicated topics, with the primary motivation to provide genuine service to its readers—and we admire that!

Introduction

While the vast majority of middle-class American households survive on two incomes, many also live on or, at the very least, experience a period when they choose or are forced to pare down to one income. In most dual-income situations, a couple decides to have children and commits to a period of time during which one parent provides full-time care. But one of the incomes can also be lost in other ways—layoffs, permanent loss of a job, relocation, health problems, divorce, the necessity of caring for an elderly parent, or family lifestyle choices. Whether or not a family has the luxury of choice, transitioning from two incomes to one creates a tangible financial challenge. Oftentimes, because couples are unaware of the real costs involved, they don't even bother to lay everything out on paper or make a plan, creating a rocky rather than a smooth transition. Relying on a vague idea or having fuzzy expectations only leads to a rude awakening. Reality often falls far short of what they thought it would be like to live on one income, leading many couples down to path to financial debacle.

One-Income Household offers concrete, easily understood financial advice and a wealth of ideas on how to survive on one income and how to transition from two incomes to one. It deals with realistic middle-class scenarios, including guidelines and worksheets tailored to really help you construct a realistic assessment of your situation, and creates a workable plan that meets your needs, protects your assets, and builds for your future—and those of your children. We provide budgeting guidelines and warnings about the pitfalls and common traps, as well as tips for ways to stay on target and save money. The book addresses individuals and families who live on one income, including those who are planning for this transition and those who are surprised by a turn of events. The advice is tailored for the layman—easy to understand, in plain and simple terms, with the upbeat attitude of "you can do it." Because you can!

The One-Income Dilemma

Chapter One

When a Divorce Plummets You into One-Income Status •
When a Stay-at-Home Mom Overspends • When a Wife Is
Caught Unaware • When a Relative Becomes Ill • When It's a
Lifestyle Choice • When a Job Suddenly Goes Away • Facing
the Challenge

IT'S NOT EASY for a couple with a combined income of $83,000 a year, making payments on a two-bedroom house in the suburbs—as well as payments on two cars, furniture, and college loans—to pare down to one income. It's hard enough to make those ends meet, let alone be able to afford the additional expenses that come with children, such as college funds and added insurance. It's a rude awakening when $83,000 drops to $45,000—or less. Many couples are caught completely unaware of the real costs and how drastically their lifestyle will change.

Even if staying home with the children is not the deciding factor, many families lose one income when layoffs or job loss occur, a job change requires relocation, one partner becomes ill, or a child or an elderly parent needs full-time care. It's not uncommon for families to coast along thinking that they are fine, but things can go wrong. It can happen in a flash—to anyone.

When a Divorce Plummets You into One-Income Status

Prior to marriage, Jennifer had worked as journalist, earning approximately $25,000 a year. When she married Edwin, he was making approximately $50,000 a year. Not long after they married, Edwin launched his own sales corporation and landed a hot line that boosted his income to as much as $300,000 a year for several years in a row. After the birth of their first child, a mere year after they married, Jennifer surrendered her full-time job and contributed to the family finances primarily through freelance work, which was unpredictable and provided income for little more than child care and clothing. After the birth of their second child, Jennifer rarely worked, except to assist Edwin, for which she did not receive a salary. Nine years later, they had two children under the age of eight and owned a $400,000 home (with $100,000 in equity) in a very upscale neighborhood.

Edwin's corporation had allowed him to determine and pay his own salary. It also allowed him and Jennifer to amass retirement funds (pre-tax) and to deduct many business expenses, such as travel, entertaining, and the costs of maintaining a home office (also pre-tax). Although they weren't set for life, everything looked rosy. All of the family's needs were met—health care, dental care, clothing, housing, transportation, and entertainment.

However, when their marriage collapsed, everything changed overnight. The business was not something that could be sold or valued, and Jennifer's role in the company had no "real" value. Edwin had established a retirement fund, but they had no other investments. Although Edwin would pay alimony for a few years, and child support until their children reached age eighteen, both amounts were based on his "income" rather than what the business brought in. Jennifer faced the sad reality that her income/lifestyle was going to plummet as much as 70 percent, while Edwin's would remain relatively the same. Jennifer had to implement immediate and tough restructuring. She needed to find a way to make significantly more money, and fast. Unfortunately, it would be virtually impossible for her to match Edwin's income, or even come close to his earning power.

Jennifer's forward motion was hampered by her need to re-enter the job market after being a stay-at-home mom for eight years, and by suddenly having to run a one-income household, which included paying for her own car, living expenses (and many of her children's), insurance, health care, and child care. Jennifer often felt completely daunted by the financial realities. Would she find a way to bolster her income? Would she be able to fund a retirement plan? Who would pay for college? Would she ever be able to save the five to six months' of reserve funds that her financial adviser suggested? For Jennifer to prosper in a one-income household, she needed to figure out the answers to some very complex problems.

When a Stay-at-Home Mom Overspends

Jane Finley is a stay-at-home mother of four children under the age of twelve. Her husband, Frank, worked as a salesman and earned $80,000–$100,000 a year. After taxes and expenses, his take-home pay ranged from $5,000–$7,000 a month. This should have been adequate for their family to lead a pretty good life in Cincinnati, but Jane and Frank made some disastrous financial decisions.

For one, they bought a brand-new, $400,000 mansion they couldn't afford for zero down and a balloon payment. Then, to "keep up with the Joneses" in their posh neighborhood, Jane bought expensive furniture on installment plans, and when she ran out of money for the month she charged everything from groceries to luxuries on their credit cards. Jane also frequently bought expensive clothing for herself and her children and showered the children with expensive gifts and extravagant birthday parties. Whatever they wanted, Jane bought. Eventually, their "credit card lifestyle" made them look far richer than they were.

Jane handled the bill paying and began juggling funds to keep her husband in the dark. When she didn't have enough money to pay all the bills or cash to spend on her many whims, Jane would write a credit-card check and take it to the bank, incurring a whopping 28 percent interest rate. When their credit cards were maxed out, Jane and Frank took out an equity loan on their house—on top of their zero down, interest-only first mortgage—which created negative amortization. In other words, their house was now worth less than they were paying for it.

When all the spending finally caught up with them, they owed almost $85,000 to eight credit card companies! This debt was in addition to two mortgages, two car leases, and an $18,000 installment loan. As their situation worsened, Jane and Frank had to swallow a bitter pill—they would have to sell the house and dramatically downsize their entire lifestyle. All those expensive luxuries that Jane craved had to be curbed, and she eventually had to take a part-time job. Naturally, this caused sleepless nights and, as the deceptions unraveled, marital discord. This stressed-out couple will need a massive intervention to conquer their debt, and then a solid budget going forward.

When a Wife Is Caught Unaware

Nancy and Joseph Banister were high school sweethearts who married as soon as Joe finished college and landed his first job. Over the years, Joe's career flourished, and their family grew. Fifteen years later, Joe, an accountant, had just opened his own office in Red Bluff, California. The couple lived in a modest but lovely house, and owned a small vacation home in the mountains. Nancy was the quintessential soccer mom, driving her four children from piano lessons to karate classes to soccer, tennis, and baseball games. Joe handled all of the bill paying and budgeting.

And then one day, tragedy struck. Joe was on his way home from visiting a client when a truck overturned and slid into Joe's car, killing him upon impact. Nancy was thirty-eight years old and a widow with four children to raise—and send to college. A few days after the funeral, when Nancy sat down with her husband's accountant, she was given more bad news.

Because Joe had recently invested a lot of money in establishing his new business, the couple's monetary reserves had been tapped. Joe had a term life insurance policy amounting to $20,000 (and they'd spent $7,000 for his burial expenses), a retirement fund of approximately $45,000, and about $9,500 in the bank. As the sole proprietor of his new business, no one was there to step into his shoes and keep the business viable.

Nancy faced a harsh reality. Her house payments were $1,620 a month, the vacation home was another $950 a month, and she had no source of income. Since Nancy had always relied on Joe, she never gained the kind of job skills that could land her a high-paying job. As a result, Nancy had to liquidate the business assets and sell the vacation house immediately, just to keep her family in their home. The proceeds would be enough to pay the bills for at least eight months, but Nancy needed a long-term plan, and she needed it fast. Nancy needed to learn financial management virtually overnight.

When a Relative Becomes Ill

Jonathan and Elizabeth Kelly, a vibrant couple in their late forties, were looking forward to the day when their children would finally be off on their own. Their eldest daughter was a junior in college, and their twins had just begun their senior year of high school. Jonathan was a high school teacher who hoped to retire in five years, when all of their children finally graduated from college. Elizabeth had a decent job as an administrative assistant in the local water works department. Between the two of them, they had a modest retirement plan and ten more years of mortgage payments. Their family functioned well and, although they lived on a tight budget, had long ago learned how to enjoy themselves without spending a lot of money.

Unfortunately, when Elizabeth's mother developed cerebral palsy, everything ground to a halt. Since Elizabeth was an only child, and her father had died a few years prior, it fell upon Elizabeth to cope with her mother's situation. After reviewing her mother's finances, it quickly became obvious that Elizabeth and Jonathan would have to take care of her. Her mother had no real assets, received less than $600 a month in social security, and would require full-time custodial care. Either Jonathan or Elizabeth would have to quit work. Since Jonathan was nearing retirement, they decided that it made more sense for Elizabeth to resign.

Suddenly their income plummeted from $72,000 a year to $47,000, and the ramifications affected the entire family. Their eldest daughter had to find a part-time job and seek financial aid to stay in college. The twins had to surrender any idea of attending a private college, and initiate their own search for financial aid for the coming year. The family also had to cut back drastically on all their creature comforts. Even with all the cost cutting, Jonathan and Elizabeth went from a comfortable lifestyle to one filled with financial setbacks and constant challenges.

When It's a Lifestyle Choice

Caitlin and Zachary Howard, a young couple expecting their first child, had decided well before getting married that once children arrived, Caitlin would stay at home to raise them. Since college, both had done well in their careers, Zachary as an account executive at an advertising firm, and Caitlin as a graphic artist for a department store. They lived in a riverfront condo in San Antonio that they had purchased two years prior. In fact, they were doing so well, they hadn't really sat down to determine how their plan would pan out.

As the due date approached, Caitlin and Zachary just assumed everything would fall into place. Caitlin handed in her resignation and began decorating their second bedroom as a nursery. Then, two weeks before the baby was scheduled to arrive, they finally sat down and reviewed their finances. Without Caitlin's $32,000 salary, they would be hard-pressed to meet all of their financial obligations, particularly the education loans and credit card debt that seemed very manageable when two incomes were coming in, but oppressive when only one had to cover everything. In addition, Zachary wanted to purchase disability insurance and life insurance to protect his growing family. When they finally added everything up, they were stunned to discover that they would be living very close to the bone. Suddenly, they realized they needed a more concrete, workable plan, and needed it fast!

When a Job Suddenly Goes Away

James and Kendra Highsmith lived in a small town in Ohio, where Kendra worked part-time as a dental assistant, earning $11,000 a year, and James worked at a local factory, earning $38,000 a year. Together, they had achieved a comfortable lifestyle that included home ownership. They had been nervous when layoffs began, but nothing prepared them for the sudden closing of the factory where James had been employed for more than ten years. One Friday, James was employed. By the next Monday, he was permanently out of a job—with six weeks severance pay, but no health insurance, no retirement fund, and no prospects.

Like millions of Americans now facing similar hardships, James and Kendra had to make immediate and radical changes in their lifestyle. Although they were lucky that Kendra still had a job, the sudden loss of income caught them unaware and unprepared. Like most middle-class families, they didn't have a huge savings account to tide them over. They had to cut all extraneous expenditures and negotiate with their creditors to lower monthly payments. By taking firm hold of their real financial situation, James and Kendra were able to forestall disaster and stay afloat—at least for a while.

If you're in this situation, Appendix A: Blindsided will both help you define your situation and take immediate and drastic action to avoid losing your home.

Facing the Challenge

Whether or not you have the luxury of planning for the drop from two incomes to one, all families who face this challenge need to create a plan that will stave off disaster—one that provides a workable budget and allows you to meet ongoing financial goals, such as saving for household repairs, replacement cars, college, retirement, or vacations. Questions you'll need to ask include these:

- What are our essential costs?
- How much can we realistically afford?
- Can we afford our current house?
- Can we afford two cars?
- How will we cover health insurance?
- Is our life insurance adequate?
- What's our overall debt situation?
- How much are our monthly credit card payments?
- How will we cut back on costs?
- How long can we survive on this income?
- How will we fund retirement?
- What are our options?
- Can we find or create additional income?

Successfully surviving—even thriving—on one income or going from two incomes to one brings harsh financial realities, but it is possible to successfully transition. If your family has the foresight to fully confront your real situation, create and follow a realistic plan, and make sacrifices, you can live on one income, or go from two incomes to one without suffering severe financial consequences. A dose of reality goes a long way, as does creating and sticking to a master plan. In an ideal world, two-income families would live on one income and save or invest the other income. Imagine how sound such a family's financial security would be, and how their asset management would contribute to our nation's economy, as well. Unfortunately, we've grown accustomed to creating dual-income families and elevating our lifestyles rather than saving as much as possible of the second income. It's also true that many need the second income to cover even basic expenses, which makes it all the harsher when that second income vanishes.

If you have suddenly been thrust into living on one income, you may find it instructive to flip to Appendix A, Blindsided: What to Do When Disaster Strikes. This appendix was designed to help a family cope when an emergency situation occurs and they have to make the shift from two incomes to one income literally overnight. Our self-described Crisis Management in a Box lays out a logical progression of all the bases you'll have to cover to stay afloat. It's designed to be a great quick reference. You'll also find helpful information in Chapter 12, Mining Your Resources. This information is designed to help those catapulted from two incomes to one virtually overnight, with no forethought or planning. If you are fortunate enough to be able to elect a smooth transition from two incomes to one, you should be able to proceed through the rest of the chapters, which provide a wealth of in-depth information on the crucial issues you will face and a lot of ideas on how to make the most of one income.

Facing Reality

Chapter Two

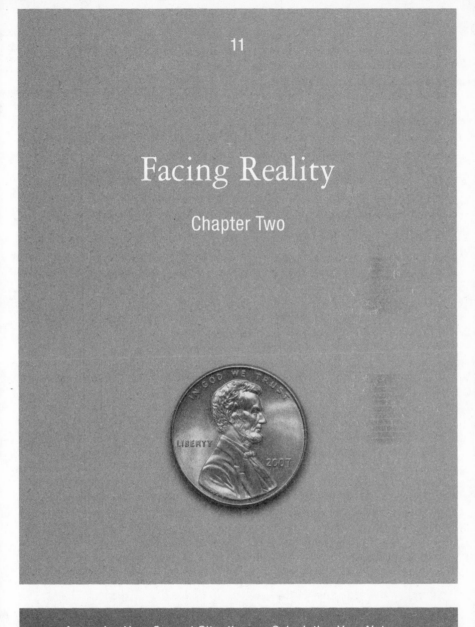

Assessing Your Current Situation • Calculating Your Net
Worth • Shining a Light in the Shadows • Making
Short-Term Decisions • Making Long-Term Decisions •
Prioritizing Savings and Investment Goals • Assuming
Fiscal Responsibility

PETER SANDER, AUTHOR of *The 250 Personal Finance Questions Everyone Should Ask*, pinpoints three characteristics that create financial success: awareness, commitment, and control. In other words, being fully conscious of your current financial reality—income, expenses, assets, and liabilities—is one key to achieving financial success. This rings even more true for a one-income household. To succeed in not only staying afloat, but thriving financially, you need to create and commit to a game plan for bolstering your income and assets, effectively managing your expenses and liabilities. Once you have a game plan, it's crucial that you make conscious decisions to do what you need to do to stay on course and that you consistently monitor your progress (which we'll discuss in greater depth in Chapter 4).

Assessing Your Current Situation

Here's what we know: Sticking your head in the sand and ignoring your financial reality will cost you money. If you want to not only survive, but to thrive, you have to start by taking stock of where you are financially, including a full and complete accounting of your income, your expenses, and your debts. You can then use this information to create a plan that takes maximum advantage of your present reality, or changes it, and moves you toward your financial goals. Do the work and financial health will come.

If you are contemplating going from two incomes to one, it's helpful if you calculate the costs that have been involved in acquiring that second income. Create two columns on a piece of paper. Above the first column write "Income" and above the second write "Expenses." Use the sample on the next page as a guideline.

The difference between the income and the expenses may not be sufficient to warrant holding on to the second income.

You should also create another two-column table reflecting the pros of keeping the second income versus the pros of flying solo. Advantages for keeping the second income may include job satisfaction, career progression, independence, an ability to make retirement fund contributions, and an ability to amass an emergency fund, among others. Advantages to living on one income might include being able to stay home with the children; being able to qualify for government assistance, low-income health insurance, or financial aid for college; being able to surrender one car; having time to learn a new skill, and so on.

INCOME	EXPENSES
Net income (after taxes and deductions)	Transportation Costs
Retirement contributions	Clothing Requirements
Medical Insurance	Day Care Expenses
	Meals Purchased at Work
	Takeout Meals Consumed at Home
	Housecleaning Service
	Dry Cleaning
	Gifts Purchased for Coworkers

Once you have completed these assessments, your next step is to calculate your net worth.

Calculating Your Net Worth

Planning your financial life without knowing your net worth is like trying to find your way into unknown territory with an out-of-date map. Even if you start taking purposeful steps in one direction, you aren't likely to end up where you want to be if you don't know exactly where you are at the moment and where you need to head.

Calculating your net worth shows you exactly where you stand financially. Your net worth is the total value of your liquid assets— cash, stock, bonds, the value of your home, and any personal property you could sell relatively quickly, such as extra cars or jewelry—minus the value of the money you owe, notably car loans, mortgages, home equity loans, furniture loans, student loans, and credit card debt. You may automatically put your car down as a valuable asset, but a car is a depreciating asset and, unless you're in the process of selling the car and won't buy a replacement, it doesn't represent cash value. This also goes for jewelry and other personal property you aren't in the process of selling. Some include the cash value of life insurance policies in the assets column, but unless you are in the process of redeeming them for cash, they may skewer your net worth calculation.

Knowledge is Power

Some 19 million middle-class Americans act as though they have incomes in the top 1 percent when they clearly do not, and an additional 20 percent think they will someday join the elite, but 99 percent will never join their ranks. Unfortunately, many Americans are increasingly unrealistic about their circumstances and their futures—they inappropriately mirror the expectations, aspirations, and spending habits of the very wealthy. (Source: Jean Chatzky, *The Ten Commandments of Financial Happiness*.)

Once you have a clear picture of what you really have, and what you really owe, you'll have a far better idea of whether you can survive on one income. It also helps you see where improvements need to happen and helps you prioritize them. The ultimate goal, of course, is to increase your assets and diminish your liabilities. You'll want to weigh how living on one income will affect your net worth, and look for ways to mitigate any negative effects.

Shining a Light in the Shadows

Now that you have a broad overview of your current financial situation, it's time to shine a light in the shadows. This will include the things you don't really want to see, such as how deeply you are in debt, how many possessions you've squandered your money to acquire, how little you have saved toward your retirement fund, and how badly you've managed money in general. It's hard to be honest about your bad habits, but failing to do so allows them to continue. To live successfully on one income, you need to own up to your bad habits and re-evaluate how you earn, spend, save, invest, and deal with money.

Begin by admitting the pitfalls you've fallen into, and then, rather than seeing them as intractable habits, see them as behaviors you need to improve. Take heart in knowing that you are not alone in sailing along without ever really questioning how you handle money. Most of us know the basic parameters of our income and our expenses, and most of us muddle along, hoping we earn enough money to cover our basic expenses and maybe enjoy life a bit. When we get a raise or some small windfall, we typically boost our standard of living rather than investing the extra sum. Only those who earn more than enough money usually have the luxury of choosing investments, or being able to afford their whims.

All of us have made financial mistakes; many have made real blunders. So go ahead, title a list "Lame Money Mistakes I Have Made," and list everything you can think of that has gobbled up potential savings, decreased your net worth, and wasted your hard-earned money. Write down all those little excesses and missteps and begin ridding them of their power to control you.

Making Short-Term Decisions

First, you really, really have to accept that absolutely everything will or has already changed. You cannot go forward with a solid base if you don't get a firm grip on what your situation is now, and begin to formulate plans for how it will look from this point forward. If you are uncertain about what to do, focus on what requires your immediate attention, such as making sure the necessities are covered, paying down your high-interest credit card, accessing your emergency fund (only if necessary), mining your resources, settling accounts you cannot afford to sustain, or simply asking for help. Some questions to ask about your short-term decisions include these:

- What are our absolute necessities?
- Who do we pay first? Who can we stall?
- How can we reduce our debt quickly?
- Where can we drastically cut expenses?
- How long can we sustain our current lifestyle?
- Do we have any assets we may want to liquidate?

As soon as you have the hot-button issues handled, it's important to give serious thought to the quality of life you want to create for yourself and your children. As it is highly likely that you'll be living on a drastically lower income, it's important to prioritize what is most important to you. Begin by making a list of what really matters in terms of lifestyle, needs, and dreams, and then keep refining and prioritizing the list until you feel it reflects who you are and the kind of life you are willing to live. To live on one income, you will undoubtedly have to make some major sacrifices, and it will be far easier to do this if you are making choices that feed your soul.

Knowledge is Power

Studies have shown that only 41 percent of Americans are better savers than spenders. Savers develop positive habits such as budgeting, tracking expenses, balancing checkbooks, paying bills as they come in, and living within or below their means. Spenders reported consistently feeling frustrated and unhappy with their circumstances.

What you are seeking is absolute clarity on who you are and how you want to live your life. While you are pondering all of this, begin taking action by making small decisions, such as relinquishing all unnecessary expenses until you achieve equilibrium, basically plugging any holes in your financial ship before it slips beneath the sea.

ONE-INCOME INQUIRY

Are You an Organizer?

According to Jean Chatzky in *The Ten Commandments of Financial Happiness*, the differences in the habits of those who employ organization to handle their finances and those who don't are striking:

Characteristic	Among Organized	Among Not-Organized
Financially secure	72%	23%
Worry about finances	56%	86%
Good money managers	61%	28%
In control of finances	73%	42%

One of the most primary ways to take responsibility for money management is to set up a system that works. If you don't already do so, select a drawer, a file holder, or a basket where you place monthly bills. Open all mail when it arrives, discard junk mail, and immediately shred all those endless credit card offers. Then, put all your bills into the designated, easily accessible drawer, file, or basket. Create a monthly payment schedule to remind you when bills are due. When bills are paid, place the statements in individual files.

You may want to consider an accounting program that is easy to use. Doing this can both simplify and benefit your bill paying. The savvier you become, the more you will be able to create reports that show you how you are doing on credit card debt, budgeting, saving, and managing your finances in general.

Making Long-Term Decisions

If you are lucky enough to have the luxury of time and sufficient assets to plan for a one-income situation, making long-term decisions will be a useful way for you to make sure that you fully understand the repercussions, how they will play out over time, and what you need to do to meet those goals.

If you were thrust unexpectedly into a one-income situation, you don't have the luxury of time and need to immediately create short-term goals and actively contemplate your long-term plan so you can make decisions that will drive a plan to achieve your long-term financial goals. These choices may be difficult to make, so begin by making a list of things you need to think about long-term and what you need to address now to make them happen. Questions you may want to answer include:

- Can you afford to stay in the house you are currently in?
- If not, how much can you afford to spend on housing?
- Where can you find housing in your price bracket?
- Can the wage earner find ways to move up at work?
- Can you find other ways to increase your income stream?
- Will the wage earner need additional education or training?
- Can you fund college for your children?
- Can you fund a savings account and/or a retirement plan?

What you're seeking is clarity about how living on one income will affect your long-term financial goals. It's important to clarify ideas about what you want to create long-term and whether you need to weigh your long-term goals when making decisions that deal with your immediate needs. For example, if you have a child who will be ready to attend college in four years, you may need to drastically cut expenses so you can channel funds into a savings plan earmarked for his or her education. This will obviously affect your short-term goals in that you will need to trim expenses further and perhaps downsize your short-term goals. In Chapter 4 we will discuss financial goals in depth, as well as how you can create concrete action plans to achieve them.

Prioritizing Savings and Investment Goals

One of the most crucial long-term decisions you can make is a commitment to establish a savings account and deposit funds on a regular basis. Ideally, you would arrange for an automatic withdrawal that plunks a set amount of funds into your savings account monthly—or weekly if possible. This habit, like no other, can brighten your future in a myriad of ways. And lest you think an established savings plan is far-fetched, consider the following illustration of how regular savings can accumulate over time.

SAVINGS GIVEN MONTHLY CONTRIBUTIONS*					
Years to spending date	$100	$200	$400	$500	$1,000
1	1,238	2,476	4,952	6,190	12,380
5	7,120	14,239	28,478	35,598	71,196
10	17,105	34,210	68,421	85,526	171,052
15	31,110	62,221	124,442	155,552	311,105
20	50,754	101,507	203,015	253,768	507,536
25	78,304	156,608	313,217	391,521	783,042

*Assumes 7% per year gains on investments after taxes

Of course most families living on one income will find it challenging to save any money, so to achieve the discipline required to achieve this goal:

- Make a commitment and stick to it.
- Regularly deposit the funds into a money market account.
- As the money grows, look for higher-return investments.

While the initial funds are accumulating, you can research investment vehicles with a higher rate of return, such as certificates of deposit (CDs), mutual funds, and bonds. Ideally, you want to achieve a return of 7 percent or more per year, averaged over time.

Assuming Fiscal Responsibility

If you want to live on one income and stay financially healthy, you need to assume a new level of fiscal responsibility. When you align your intention with your values, and establish habits that coincide with your desired outcome—in essence living the decision—the universe (and your own subconscious) lays the groundwork for making it a reality. So decide, and get cracking on making your desired outcome a reality. Follow the seven basic rules that follow, and you'll be well on your way.

1. *Accept responsibility for your financial future.* You are responsible for making sure that you—and your family—are financially secure. Commit fully to your financial plan of action. Review your short-term financial goals quarterly, and your long-term goals annually.
2. *Pay yourself first.* Having an emergency fund and a retirement fund will protect you from financial hurricanes. If at all possible, unfailingly and automatically deposit 10 percent of your paycheck into your savings.
3. *Stay fully conscious of your financial situation.* Don't pull the wool over your own eyes. Know what and how you are doing financially at all times.

4. *Reduce spending.* Instead of spending, get your kicks from saving. Separate essential expenses from expendable expenses, and channel whatever you can into your savings or retirement fund—and pat yourself on the back for doing so.

5. *Earn more at your job.* Commit to being more competent at work by acquiring new skills or expanding your field of responsibility. Rather than resting comfortably, think progressively.

6. *Generate additional income streams.* Keep your eyes open for opportunities to generate additional income streams—whether capitalizing on hobbies such as photography or furniture refinishing or pie baking or any unique skills you (or your spouse) may have that are marketable or that can produce a marketable product, or, if at all possible, assist in finding a second job.

7. *Invest wisely.* Make the most of your savings by investing as much as you can in tax-deferred savings accounts such as a 401(k) or an IRA.

Adjusting Your Attitude

Chapter Three

Money Attitudes That Sabotage You • Surrender the "Can-Have" Attitude • Steer Clear of Madison Avenue • Think Like a Millionaire • Unveil Hidden Money Attitudes • Surrender Your Two-Income Mindset • Where to Begin Again?

THE FINANCIAL HEALTH of many families has worsened over the last few years. People have found it harder and harder to get jobs, and foreclosures and high housing costs make it impossible for some to keep their homes. Energy costs are skyrocketing, driving up the price of transportation, travel, even groceries. It has become very hard for one-income households to weather inflationary costs eating away their hard-earned income. When you're in that sort of white-knuckle existence, it's time to rethink your money attitudes.

Money Attitudes That Sabotage You

In our culture, we tend to measure our intrinsic value by our earning potential, how much money our parents had, how much money we have, the size of our houses or cars, the clothing we wear, the vacations we take, or our bank balances. To successfully live on one income, it becomes highly important for you to sift through the cultural, familial, and personal myths that may be undermining your own feelings of self-worth, and how they can, or already have, become deeply intertwined with how you handle your money.

Like Jane and Frank, the couple mentioned in Chapter 1 who were living the high life without establishing a real financial base or making sound financial decisions, people who are living beyond their real means are not wealthy in any sense of the word. Living in a bigger house than you can afford, purchasing fancy furniture, showy furnishings, or china, driving expensive cars, wearing expensive clothing or accessories, or regularly indulging in extravagance may give the appearance of wealth, but in reality depletes your opportunity to attain genuine wealth. The thrill is short-lived and you're left holding nothing of real value in your hands. If you are frittering your money away on transient possessions or an indulgent lifestyle, you may not have enough money to adequately pay your bills, make any sound investments that could build wealth, or achieve true financial security. The only things worth spending money on are a house you can afford, your retirement fund, your children's education, absolute necessities (gas, heat, electricity, health care, and so on), and smart investments. This is a very important concept to understand: True wealth is based not on how much you can spend, but on how much money you can actually accumulate.

Knowledge is Power	With the advent of credit cards in the 1970s, Americans embraced immediate gratification—we love believing that we deserve to have what we want, when we want it, whether or not we have the money to pay for it. Our grandparents didn't have that cultural attitude. They bought what they needed only when they had cash to pay for it, and rarely indulged in buying things they didn't need. We have all been led to believe that we can afford to use credit cards or borrow money to get what we want, and advertisers have become very rich by preying upon our insecurities.

Surrender the "Can-Have" Attitude

In recent years, many Americans have developed a "can-have" culture instead of a "can-do" attitude. Yes, you can lease a fancy BMW for a few thousand down and the same monthly payment you would make to own another, more sensible car; yes, you can open up five new credit card accounts and keep shuffling charges onto them; yes, you can have a house with no money down and zero interest for the first three years. What we seem to fail to realize is that each "yes" contains a huge, though all-too-often unspoken and unacknowledged "but": But you will end up making substantial payments for the leased car and not own it in five years; but you will run out of credit and have to pay all those transferred balances at some point; but the mortgage that looked so attractive will go up substantially in three to five years, and you may not be able to make the payments.

You may not be addicted to cigarettes, alcohol, or pain pills, but you may be addicted to overspending or posturing, which may mask feelings of inferiority in an attempt to stave off the fear of being "less than." On some level, many of us in the middle or working class have come to believe that we're not complete, worthy human beings unless we have achieved a certain status in terms of looks, money, or possessions.

ONE-INCOME INQUIRY

What's the difference between cost and value?

There is a vast difference between value and cost. Cheap things don't age well, which means they have little to no value. Even if it costs more money, a product's value equates to how long it lasts and how little it costs to maintain. For example, if you save $300 on a cheap refrigerator and it breaks down within two years, your savings are likely to be annihilated, particularly if you could have paid only slightly more for an energy-efficient, higher-quality fridge. Sometimes it makes more sense to spend more for intrinsic value. When it comes to big-ticket items, weigh the value versus the cost carefully.

Steer Clear of Madison Avenue

As a nation, we have become highly susceptible to—and are constantly bombarded by—advertising, which delights the people running the large advertising and marketing agencies lining Madison Avenue, one of the wealthiest streets in our country. The owners of those firms hire the best market analysts available to manipulate our tender psyches. If you are driving, walking, running, or crawling anywhere with at least one eye open, you are being courted by advertisers, visually and often subliminally.

When it comes to car ads, for example, advertisers focus on the monthly payment versus the total price, inclusive of the interest rate you would pay. That sleek new car that they virtually promise will transform your image doesn't cost $38,000; it only costs $592 a month—and you don't have to make a down payment! What you often have to do is pay that $592 a month for seven years (or more) instead of a more affordable five years, and pay a higher interest rate than you would if you made a 20 percent down payment, had an excellent credit rating, and could truly afford the car. Let's not even discuss leasing a fancy car, which for the vast majority of us is like throwing money down a drain.

Advertisers have become highly adept at convincing us that owning expensive possessions makes us sexy, alluring, confident, and happy. If you really stop to think about it, that message doesn't make any sense at all. Nevertheless, most of us are guilty of trading our hard-won money for an expensive new car, a few weeks of pleasure, or a boatload of unnecessary goods or services that ultimately leave us anxious and depressed by the voluminous debt we now carry on our backs. Our contemporary culture sells the belief that owning certain "stuff"— whether it's trendy, brand-new mountain bikes, an SUV, a 54-inch HDTV, a Bose home theater system, a diamond Cartier watch, or a vastly overpriced designer handbag—guarantees social acceptance. Ironically, when we go into debt to obtain those lifestyle markers, we raise the odds that we'll never actually be rich. Rather than succumb to the fantasy that advertising agencies dangle in front of your eyes, never trade tomorrow's financial independence in a feeble, unnecessary attempt to keep up with your boss, coworkers, friends, or neighbors.

Think Like a Millionaire

Contrary to what you might imagine, most millionaires don't live an opulent lifestyle, wear flashy clothes, or buy flashy cars. Those who chase the image of status are usually people who sell things to rich people but aren't actually rich themselves. In fact, consider these interesting and eye-opening statistics about American millionaires, taken from *The 5 Lessons a Millionaire Taught Me About Life and Wealth*, by Richard Paul Evans:

- The median income for American millionaires is $131,000.
- 97 percent own their own homes.
- The average value of their house is $320,000.
- About half have lived in the same house for twenty years or more.
- Fewer than one in four millionaires own a new car.
- Fewer than one in five leases a car.
- The average price they paid for a car is slightly less than $25,000.
- For more than one-third, their most recent purchase was a used car.
- Only 6.4 percent drove a Mercedes or a Lexus. Less than 3 percent drive a Jaguar.
- 60 percent drive an American car.
- 50 percent never paid more than $400 for a suit in their lives, for themselves or anyone else.
- About half never paid more than $140 for a pair of shoes.

Knowledge is Power

If you strongly suspect that you've been living beyond your means, compulsively overspending, or even simply undersaving, Stacy Johnson, author of *Life or Debt: A One-Week Plan for a Lifetime of Financial Freedom*, recommends keeping the following in mind:

- It's not having enough money that sets us free; it's having no debt. The people who have more money than they'll ever need and the people who don't owe anyone anything are the only ones free to do what they want.
- The decisions you make about borrowing and spending have a far-reaching, inclusive effect on your quality of life. Living life without debt means you are free to pursue your passion.
- The more things you buy, the more tied down you become. Some people become prisoners of their possessions, instead of the other way around.

Unveil Hidden Money Attitudes

Without question, money talks. Even if your grandparents, parents, or extended family never discussed money in front of you, their financial status, attitudes, and behaviors spoke volumes. If your parents handled their finances well, you've probably learned how to budget, create short- and long-term goals, and to save and invest your money. However, if your parents didn't handle money well, you may lack budgeting skills, be more impulsive and reactionary when it comes to handling money, and have a lot of negative impressions or habits—including an underlying fear that the financial rug could be pulled out from under you at any point.

To probe your family's underlying money attitudes, take a few moments to answer the following questions:

- Were your grandparents financially secure? How about your parents?
- If yes, did they make solid investments and build toward financial wealth, or were they focused on appearing rich?
- If not, did they accept that they would never have money and do nothing to alter their fate?
- Were they solidly middle class, or barely able to survive financially?
- Did they fear poverty and hoard their money rather than invest it?
- Did they spend lavishly or only spend when absolutely necessary?
- When they talked about money, did it ultimately lead to worried whispers or shouting matches?
- Did they successfully budget money, or were they constantly bouncing checks?
- Who handled the household money? Was that person successful or irresponsible?
- Did either partner hide bad habits from his or her spouse?
- Was the father automatically in charge?
- Were negative attitudes portrayed about women and their ability to earn or manage money?

- Did they teach you how to save money, create a budget, spend money conservatively, and/or invest money?
- What underlying feelings and beliefs either positively or negatively established your attitudes about money?

This next step can really help you understand how your attitudes took shape—and how you can transform them. Even though you may question its usefulness, write a short, but well-thought-out financial biography that captures your cultural and familial climate as you grew up. Focus on how the presence of, absence of, obsession with, or disregard for money affected you socially, physically, emotionally, and spiritually. Did your family have plenty of money, or were they constantly living on the brink of financial disaster? What effects did a lower- or middle-class background have on your family's financial undercurrents? As a child, did you feel spoiled, entitled, secure, tenuous, poor, or on the brink of living in the streets? Did you grow up vowing to be more educated, richer, smarter, more ambitious, more adventurous, or more conservative than your parents? When you began earning and spending your own money, did you feel guilty, remorseful, or afraid when you spent large amounts? Did you start off consistently spending more than you could afford? When you landed your first job, did you automatically open a savings account? When you think about money, does it thrill you or chill you?

As you work your way through this exercise and probe deeply into your financial past, your self-examination will lead to priceless self-knowledge and a renewed and original method of making solid financial choices.

Surrender Your Two-Income Mindset

If both of your parents worked, or if you and your partner/spouse have grown accustomed to two incomes, you will need to consciously surrender your two-income mindset. Basically, until World War II, when vast numbers of women entered the work force, most families relied on one income. After World War II, as more and more women stayed in the work force, families ratcheted up their lifestyle and soon began to rely on two incomes for basic survival. At first, it seemed a fabulous way to afford a better house, better cars, a more luxurious lifestyle, and so on. However, relying upon two incomes also set the bar high. Once you've grown accustomed to being able to afford more, it's hard to cut back to one income.

Knowledge is Power

The Employee Benefit Research Institute (EBRI) publishes research on the economic security of American workers. They found that credit card usage has skyrocketed. People are going deeply into debt for things that they used to pay for in cold hard cash—even cars and college! Also, although many Americans are doing better given the recent financial climate, in 2005 the national savings rate was zero. This compared poorly to Europeans who saved 10 percent and Italians who saved 16 percent of their household income in 2005.

Ideally, families would rely on one income, and if they had two incomes, would use the second income to make investments, accumulate savings, or fatten their retirement funds. Unfortunately, for the vast majority of lower- and middle-class families, it's become increasingly hard to survive on one income, and impossible to adequately fund their retirement, save money, and pay off their houses or cars. Increasingly, lower- and middle-class families struggle to stay afloat. That said, it is possible to survive on one income, and we'll spend the remainder of the book giving you numerous, very concrete strategies for doing so. Begin, however, with adjusting your mindset.

When you first go from a two-income to a one-income household, your perspective on everything is skewed. It's time to think outside the box when it comes to how you view and manage money. Rather than falling prey to the mindset that you can have it all, you need to set more realistic financial expectations. Sort out what you really believe—or what you want to work toward believing. For example, rather than caring so much about a large house in an expensive neighborhood, embrace the charm of a smaller house in an "emerging neighborhood." In many regions of Europe, for example, families live in cramped spaces and acquire few possessions. Instead they buy far fewer, but higher-quality clothes, treasure "antique" furniture that is not beautifully restored, tend to live closer to where they work, and shop local markets, only buying what they need for that day and the next. If you decide to make these changes, you can downsize both your expectations and your spending habits and experience a marvelous life, full of good times and prosperity. Consider your new way of thinking about and handling money as a grand plan rather than a punishing one.

Knowledge is Power	According to David Bach, author of *Smart Women Finish Rich,* 90 percent of women will have sole responsibility for their finances at some point. Three out of four people living in poverty are women, and seven out of ten women will live in poverty at some point in their lives.

Where to Begin Again?

Sometimes we are thrown into singledom, often against our wishes, and often with dire consequences. Your spouse may suddenly die from a heart attack, traffic accident, or other cause, and leave you responsible for keeping the family or yourself afloat. Or perhaps your spouse secretly decides that he or she is in love with someone else and files for divorce. No matter how it happens, spouses or partners frequently find themselves on their own again. Even if you came out of the death, divorce, or separation with a comfortable cushion of money and assets, you will now be fully responsible for all financial decisions that will directly affect you—and perhaps your children—for decades to come. If you are not money-savvy, this could cause massive anxiety, or lead to impulsive decisions that undermine your long-term security. Take time to gather yourself and start afresh.

To begin, it's important to take a hard look at your most recent financial partnership and see how both of you handled two incomes. This means exploring your financial history—how you were doing before you coupled, and how you have done since coupling. Examine how your partner impacted your thoughts about money, solvency, investments, and how you handled money in general. Use the following questions as a starting point:

- What were your financial failings or weaknesses?
- What drove you crazy regarding your spouse's financial habits prior to marriage?
- Were you happier spending or saving?
- What really made *you* happy?
- After marriage, who took the financial reins and why?
- Did you truly feel that you made good decisions?
- Did you and your spouse want the same things from the family finances?
- What did you learn from his or her mistakes and his or her successes?
- What would you have done differently?

When you've cleared the decks of negative beliefs or limitations imposed by others, you create opportunities for new thoughts and beliefs to form. These new beliefs will become the cornerstone of your new financial philosophy, which will set things in motion and lead to a concrete action plan to help you successfully live on one income. From this point on, you'll reorder your financial priorities and position yourself on more solid financial ground. Give yourself kudos for taking the first true steps to improving your financial decisions. Repeat this as your new financial mantra: I am reordering my financial universe, and I *will* soon reap the rewards.

Making a Plan

Chapter Four

Why Goals Will Save Your Sanity • Establish Long-Term Goals • Establish Short-Term Goals • Funding Retirement • The Rules of Engagement • Taking the Fiscal Reins • Checklist

IN THE PREVIOUS chapters, you did the necessary work to create a clear picture of your current financial situation and what needs to be done. Now you are ready to take the next step: to gain control of your personal finances by creating meaningful, achievable, and time-based financial goals. Once you've established your financial priorities, you need to create a comprehensive game plan for achieving them within your time frame. The hardest part will be sticking to the strictures required to realize long-term goals—keeping your eye on a dream that seems far away, and may continue to seem far away for a long time.

Why Goals Will Save Your Sanity

According to David Bach's *Smart Women Finish Rich*, a forty-year-old Harvard study followed the progress of students who graduated in 1953. Only 3 percent of these participants reported that they actually wrote down specific goals and created plans to achieve them. By 1973, the 3 percent who recorded their goals accumulated more wealth than the remaining 97 percent of their class combined.

Establishing financial goals will help you survive on one income and help you make the best use of your available resources. Your primary goal will be to afford your lifestyle, while protecting your—and your children's—future. In other words, you need to establish goals that will help you stay on course. Without goals we are rudderless. And when you are a one-income household, having clear, concrete, realistic goals will help you live within your means and save for your future. Goals will keep you on the path to success, whereas not having goals will lead down a self-defeating path. As you work toward setting your goals, there are specific tasks that should be among them, such as creating an emergency fund, establishing short-term and long-term goals, and creating a workable budget. We'll discuss these specific tasks in depth in the following sections.

Create an Emergency Fund

One of your first goals should be to accumulate an emergency fund. Every financial adviser in the world stresses this point, and every struggling family finds it extremely difficult to amass one month's living expenses, let alone three to five months' expenses to deposit in a savings account! Nevertheless, having an emergency fund will provide important protection for your one-income household. One-income households are more vulnerable than two-income families precisely because they are dependent upon one income. If the provider becomes ill or disabled, the family can plummet into a financial disaster zone within days. Even if you have disability insurance, myriad things can happen that will require cash on hand. Make it your first short-term goal to create an "emergency" savings account of at least two months' salary. This cash pillow should be at the top of your goals and requisite before you address investing.

Establish Long-Term Goals

Long-term goals often require an ability to expend energy on a series of smaller goals that build upon each other and inch you ever closer to your ultimate goals. These long-term goals are really your dreams—the circumstances you want to create that will bring you inner happiness—but they require a belief that you'll get there eventually.

To create long-term goals, you need to give serious thought to what you want to achieve for yourself and your family in the next ten to twenty years. Whether it's paying off your house, accumulating two college funds, or building a business, long-term goals require both effort and patience. They can also be extraordinary motivators and offer some of life's most precious rewards. Everyone needs a dream. Your one-income household must have both a game plan for immediate needs and a vision for long-term needs, wants, or desires. Long-term goals can be the compass that keeps you on course.

Knowledge
is Power

Prioritize your goals. If you have massive credit card debt, or delinquent accounts, addressing these crisis situations needs to be a top priority. The cost of carrying high-interest debt will defeat long-term goals before you get them off the ground. Once you've vanquished the debt dragon, you can refocus your goals on savings and wealth creation.

For example, if your goal is to pay off your mortgage by the time your first child will begin college, you need to figure out exactly what needs to be done to achieve the goal. Perhaps it will require one additional payment a year, or paying twice a month instead of once a month.

If you have disposable income and no higher-interest debts, paying off your mortgage ahead of time is a fabulous long-term goal. If you've just purchased a home using a 30-year mortgage charging 9 percent interest, you can end your loan in twenty-two years by paying 8.5 percent more than the minimum payment. You can pay off your 15-year mortgage in twelve years by paying an extra 13 percent over the minimum.

To meet these additional payments, you may have to slash your budget, have a garage sale twice a year, or add a part-time job. Just having the long-term goal in sight helps you focus your energy and think outside the box. You can meet financial goals while living on one income; you just need to break them down into manageable bites and take prudent action to set them in motion. In essence, you would make finding that extra 8.5 or 13 percent a short-term goal for each year, which in turn would advance your long-term goal. If those amounts are too high, adjust your goal to something more achievable.

Establish Short-Term Goals

Short-term goals are manageable goals you can achieve in a relatively short amount of time. Paying down all of your credit card debt, paying off a furniture or car loan, and establishing a savings account to cover your emergency fund or to pay for a new refrigerator are all short-term goals. As long as you create them and set a viable deadline for achieving them, you're on the right track. Short-term goals should be:

- **Specific.** Be clear and straightforward when setting short-term goals and break them down into their smallest denominator to increase the likelihood of meeting them.
- **Measurable.** Make sure they provide quantifiable, visible results within a self-determined, relatively short time frame.
- **Attainable.** You want to reach a little, but not so far that you can't meet them relatively quickly.
- **Valuable.** If your goals are in alignment with your values, you'll feel good about working toward them.
- **Progressive.** They should advance your long-term goals or build upon each other to advance your cause.
- **Primary.** Start with those that will guarantee success and motivate you to solidify a practice of setting and achieving short-term goals.

People often confuse short-term goals with a "to do" list, but a short-term goal is a bar you set for yourself that achieves something of value. They may require a "to do" list, but rather than feeling relieved when you reach a true short-term goal, you feel enthusiasm and excitement. For example, if your short-term goal is to organize your bill-paying procedure, your "to do" list may include these steps: (1) buying filing folders; (2) separating bills, bank statements, loan statements, investment statements, tax returns, and so on; (3) filing the physical copies in clearly marked folders; (4) researching and buying a budget-tracking software program; (5) entering all the data that will allow you to stay on top of your monthly finances; and (6) creating a monthly calendar that reminds you when bills are due. You'll be relieved as each task is done, but when you have all six tasks completed, you'll feel elated because you are more in control of what's happening, and you'll be motivated to reach for the next short-term goal—such as learning about and saving up to purchase bonds.

Knowledge
is Power ◀ According to Glinda Bridgforth and Gail Perry-Mason in *Girl, Get Your Money Straight*, goals need clarity *and* visibility. Once you define what you want, why you want it, when you want it, and how to get it, write specific, measurable, and achievable goals. Create target dates and a list of tasks required. Then place a list of your goals in places you frequent—your bedroom, your home office, your refrigerator—so that the daily reminder will spur conscious efforts *and* inspire your unconscious energy to work its magic.

When creating short-term and long-term goals, accentuate the positive. The whole point of making goals is to create a positive vision of your future. If goals are conceived as punishment, you won't be inspired to achieve them. Instead of writing "I won't screw up paying my bills again," write "I am choosing to be proactive in getting a handle on my everyday finances." You don't need another opportunity for self-flagellation; what you need is empowerment!

Create a Workable Budget

Creating and sustaining a workable budget should be at the top of your short-term goal list. Budgeting, like dieting, is all about shedding unhealthy, nonproductive, ultimately punitive habits and replacing them with healthy, productive, far more satisfying habits. You have to relearn money basics—like how to pay the essential bills first, how to live within your means, how to maximize expenditures, and how to save. Just as mindlessly consuming empty calories can make you fat, mindlessly spending money you don't really have can make you broke. Just as you can't cinch in the belt and make yourself thin, you can't cinch in your spending habits and make yourself rich. And just as you have to relearn how to eat when dieting, you have to re-learn how to spend—or not to spend—when budgeting. It's not a *let's tighten our belts for a few months* mentality, it's *let's rethink our habits, attitudes, and behaviors, and make a real change.*

When preparing a workable budget, you have to spend the necessary time to really sort out your income and expenses, and learn what is most valuable to you. You'll never be happy if you have to deny yourself the opportunity to enjoy the things that bring you the most pleasure. What a workable budget does is create a system for paying all the necessary bills, padding your savings, creating an emergency fund, and allowing for the occasional indulgence. What you want to do is to prioritize your needs and your wants. You may have to be clever when it comes to fulfilling those wants, but it's never healthy to attempt to totally deny them.

COMPUTE YOUR INCOME

When creating a budget, you first want to compute your income. List all the sources and amounts of money coming into your household. This includes your normal paycheck amount (minus taxes, social security, retirement fund, and other deductions), additional income (if you have a part-time job or occasional freelance work or an inheritance or financial gifts that come in regularly), interest, and dividends. It's highly important that you use your after-tax income amount. We are fond of quoting our gross income (before tax and retirement and health care deductions), but that isn't really what we have to spend. If your income keeps a fairly steady pace, use your last year's income tax return to acquire your net pay amount and then divide that by twelve. Compare that number with what you are bringing home today. Keep in mind, however, that saving the amount of a raise or other increase in your income is an excellent way to accrue an emergency fund or invest in your retirement fund.

COMPUTE YOUR EXPENSES

There are basically two types of expenses: fixed expenses and variable expenses. Fixed expenses are expenses that don't tend to fluctuate in timing or amount. Your fixed expenses probably include these:

- Savings
- Mortgage payment or rent
- Common charges or condo fees
- Home equity or line of credit payments
- Child support or alimony payments
- Car payments
- Utilities: electric, gas, water, garbage
- Cable television and/or Internet expenses
- Telephone: landlines and cell phones
- Insurance: house, automobile, health, dental, life, and disability
- Student loans
- Outstanding long-term debt, such as loans for furniture, appliances, and so on
- Commuting expenses: train, subway, carpool, tolls, etc.
- College tuition, if appropriate

Variable expenses are those that may or may not occur regularly, but have a fluctuating amount. Some examples of variable expenses include:

- Credit card debt
- Groceries
- Car maintenance: gas, oil, checkups, tires, and repairs
- Home maintenance: everything from small repairs to a new roof
- Health care expenses that come out of your pocket
- Child care or baby-sitting expenses
- Clothing, shoes, and clothing upkeep

- Expenditures at work: coffee, lunches, snacks, drinks after work, etc.
- Furnishings and appliances
- Personal care expenses: haircuts, beauty products, manicures, etc.
- Christmas, birthday, special occasion gifts
- Recreation: movies, theater, dining out, etc.
- Entertaining, such as dinner or birthday parties you host
- Expenses related to your children's activities, summer camp, sports, etc.
- Hobbies: What you spend on books, classes, materials, etc.
- Vacations
- Pet food, veterinarian expenses, grooming, and boarding

Even though these lists are extensive, you will find that you spend money on many things that are difficult to pinpoint, such as coffee at your favorite coffee shop, the occasional concert, a new blender, newspapers, or magazines. If you have a realistic picture of what you spend, write it all down immediately. If you don't have a clear idea of what you actually spend your money on, carry a notebook around for a month and write down every penny you spend and what you spent it on.

Balance Your Budget

For our immediate purposes, once you've made these lists, subtract your total expenses from your income. The number now staring you in the face is either your profit or your loss. For most of us, that number is probably a loss, or at least a near dip into the red zone. If you're lucky enough to have a profit, you are living within your means. However, if that's the case, it's important to make sure that you've added in a retirement fund, regular savings, and the creation of an emergency fund that will not be touched for normal expenses. If you're in the red, or if your profit provides too narrow of a margin, do whatever it takes to balance your budget. Most likely you will need to find multiple ways to tighten your financial belt and reduce your expenses.

Remember, even if you're in the red and can only inch yourself slowly upward, you still need an additional amount allocated for regular savings and an emergency fund. Ideally, you'd save at least 10 percent of your monthly income and would have enough money in an emergency account to cover expenses for at least three, but preferably five months. You may have to bite the bullet and pare down expenses until you can fund these two aspects of your financial base.

A workable budget requires that you set parameters for what you can afford to spend and then adhere to them. Budget for your necessities first, and then prioritize expenses in order of importance. Budgets don't have to be written in stone, but staying within the parameters means that you can afford what you are spending your money on, and it keeps you out of financial trouble. Regularly review your budget to make necessary adjustments.

Funding Retirement

Although your budget is likely to be stretched, it is always important that you make funding your retirement plan a priority. Even if your employer offers a retirement plan, you may want to establish a second retirement fund for your nonworking spouse or partner. Because it can be a daunting task not only to save but also to know how much to save, we've created a detailed calculator in Appendix B that provides clear-cut instructions for determining your retirement needs.

Basically, anyone who can afford to do so should create and continuously add to a retirement fund. Even if your employer offers a plan, any extra funds you can contribute will go a long way toward ensuring your health and well-being down the road. It can also offer extra protection for your partner. The younger you are, the easier it will be to begin. There are tables in Appendix B that illustrate how saving a little can build into substantial sums over the years.

The Rules of Engagement

As a one-income household, it's extremely important that you create a budget that keeps your spending in line and that also funds your safety nets. Unless your income is well above average, you'll likely be pinching pennies, at least for a while. To succeed, you'll need to make sure everyone in the family is on board, and that means both spouses, if you are married, and all of your children. Once you know what you have to do, it's helpful to sit down with the entire family to discuss the changes you are putting in place.

If you have been living a more expensive lifestyle, you'll need to explain to your children why you are tightening the belt. You don't want to issue dire news or alarm them in any way, but you will be teaching your children valuable lessons about money management if you explain the basic concept of living within your means, setting goals, and budgeting to meet them. If you explain this in a way that makes sense and inspires them, you will likely find them eager participants. You can even make it a game by asking them to share their ideas about ways the family can save money or earn extra money. Children can be very inventive and cooperative. Making charts that remind everyone about the family rules and that illustrate progress can keep your family fully conscious, enthused, and ever mindful of the goals you are working to achieve.

Once a month, review the rules, chart your success, and celebrate the family's cooperative efforts with a special, affordable treat, such as a video night or dinner at your favorite pizza parlor.

Taking the Fiscal Reins

Now that you've established long-term and short-term goals, created a workable budget, initiated an emergency fund, and—ideally—created a retirement fund, it's highly important that you take the fiscal reins to execute your plans. Taking action is paramount, but it's also important that you monitor and evaluate your progress. We suggest a monthly review of the budget to pinpoint problems and self-correct. If you find that you simply can't fit everything in, force yourself to make some tough choices to bring your budget back into balance. If you find a surplus (marvelous surprise!), allocate it to savings and pat yourself on the back.

If you don't quite meet some of your short-term goals, you may feel like you failed. However, when working toward your long-term goals, the beauty of "failing" to reach short-term goals is that even if you only accomplish a fraction of the long-term, you've won. "Failure" in this context is normal. At the very least, you have become far more conscious of your financial realities, and taking financial responsibility is a huge success. Instead of second-guessing yourself, or abandoning the plan, evaluate whether you set your initial goals too high.

It's advisable to review your progress toward short-term goals at least every three months. Some questions to ask include these:

- Are your short-term goals effectively working toward your long-term goals? If not, what needs to be changed?
- Are you making the returns on your investments that are necessary to meet your long-term goals? If returns have been falling short, you need to either save more or find a higher-return investment to meet your goals.
- What caused the missteps? Did you miss your savings hurdle because of unexpected one-time expenses, or because you fell off the budget wagon? What do you need to do to get back on course?

If you have reached some, or all, of your short-term goals, create a new set of logically ordered, short-term goals that will maintain the momentum. If you have fallen off the budget wagon, figure out how to avoid making the same mistake again. Make any adjustments that you need to make to target and eradicate problems, and to bolster your fiscal health.

The review process helps you—and your children, if they are participating—recognize your progress. And, by all means, celebrate the milestones, no matter how small. If you have taken the reins by creating goals and working to achieve them, you are on your way to financial health. That's quite an accomplishment for a one-income household.

Checklist

Now we suggest that you create a checklist that will help you monitor your financial plan and stay on track. We've provided the following list as a guideline. Take heart in knowing that we'll be guiding you through the various tasks listed throughout the book, and that this checklist is solely meant to be a guide for you to develop your own checklists. Extrapolate the ideas that will work for your situation to create your own checklist, and then use it, preferably every three months, to review your financial progress. When you discover shortfalls, you can adjust your plan to move in the desired direction. Also, as you grow used to the process, you'll gain not only valuable wisdom, but increased motivation and satisfaction. It feels good to be able to support your family on one income and to do so successfully. Not only can you achieve this, but adopting all of these positive and responsible behaviors will help you learn to build wealth, ultimately securing your—and your children's—future.

ATTITUDES

❑ Have I reviewed my family history in relation to money?

❑ Have I separated fact from fantasy?

❑ Have I established new opinions and beliefs?

❑ Am I forging my own money mentality?

❑ Have I ventured beyond my comfort zone to make an investment?

❑ Have I identified and adjusted any fears or negative ideas that would hold me back?

❑ Am I wealth-oriented?

ORGANIZATION

❑ Do I use a software program or my own organizational method to stay on top of my finances?

❑ Do I monitor our spending and readjust our budget as needed?

❑ Do I review all of our bills to check for accuracy?

❑ Do I regularly review credit card bills to see the interest rate?

❑ Do I have a filing system for important financial documents?

❑ Do I collect, sort, and file information needed for tax preparation?

GOALS

❑ Have I created a series of realistic short-term goals?

❑ Have I created a series of realistic long-term goals?

❑ Have I instituted changes to meet my goals?

❑ Do I review my goals periodically?

REAL ESTATE

- ❑ Am I living in a house I can afford?
- ❑ Am I making my payments on time?
- ❑ Am I paying 10 percent extra toward my mortgage every month?
- ❑ Am I paying off my equity loan or line of credit?
- ❑ Am I maintaining my property?
- ❑ Do I have sufficient insurance?

SAVINGS

- ❑ Have I opened a money market account for savings?
- ❑ Have I sufficiently funded my emergency savings (at least three months' expenses)?
- ❑ Am I making regular contributions to my savings?
- ❑ Do I have my employer automatically deduct 10 percent that goes into my savings?
- ❑ Once I have enough funds, am I choosing investments that make my money grow?

INSURANCE

- ❑ Do I have health insurance for my children and myself?
- ❑ Do I have dental insurance for my children and myself?
- ❑ Do I have sufficient life insurance?
- ❑ Are my children listed as beneficiaries on my life insurance?
- ❑ Do I regularly review my home and car insurance?

WILLS

- ❑ Have I chosen guardians and/or custodians for my children?
- ❑ Have I prepared a formal will?
- ❑ Have I listed my spouse and/or my children as my beneficiaries?

Digging Out

Chapter Five

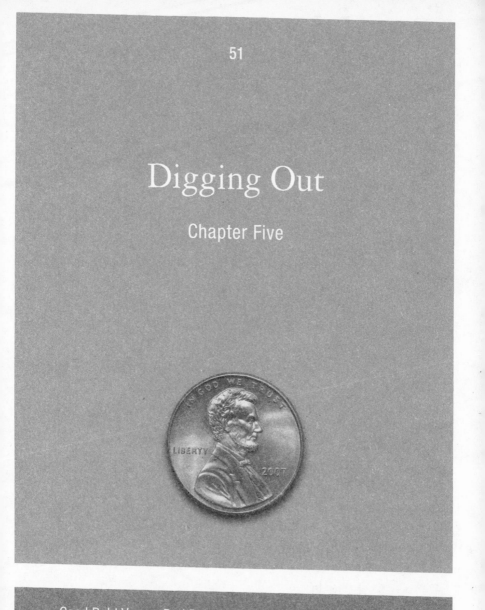

Good Debt Versus Bad Debt • Why We Have Become a Credit Card Nation • Avoid Department Store Credit Cards • Create a Game Plan to Reduce Debt • Institute a Plan to Pay Down Your Debt • Debt Management Programs • Avoid "High-Risk" Borrowing to Pay Down Debts • Should I Settle Old Accounts? • Develop a Cash Mentality

WHEN YOU BEGIN living on one income, managing debt will become crucial to your continued financial health. If you are like many Americans, you are probably carrying more debt than you'd prefer, and may have more than you can handle. Some estimates say Americans owe $1.7 trillion dollars in personal debt, and that one-third of that is credit card debt.

Good Debt Versus Bad Debt

Not all debt is bad; in fact, there is such a thing as good debt. It's important to make smart money decisions by differentiating between good and bad debts—maximizing one and minimizing the other. But the cardinal rule is that your total debt payments should not exceed 36 percent of your total gross income; this includes payments on your house, car, insurance, medical bills, credit cards, and student loans.

Basically, when a debt vastly increases the actual amount to be paid for a product that is not going to increase in value, it's a bad debt. When debt is used purposefully and intelligently to build wealth by buying something that will increase in value over time beyond the cost of carrying the debt, such as to invest in a house or a solid business venture, it's a profitable or good debt. Let's look at some examples of bad and good debt:

- Suppose you buy clothing on a credit card, or furniture by acquiring a loan. The product either immediately goes down in value (because it becomes "used") or has no potential to gain in value, yet the purchase requires you to make payments at high interest rates over a long period of time. In this case you've created a bad debt.
- If you borrow to buy something that will result in increased value or that will increase your earning power—student loans, real estate loans, home mortgages, and business loans, for example—it is considered good debt.

- Debts that are tax-deductible, such as second mortgages, equity loans, or equity lines of credit, are also good debts, provided you keep them manageable and repay them as soon as possible.

Taking a second mortgage to pay down credit card debt can turn bad debt into good debt, particularly if you obtain a home equity loan with a tax-deductible, low interest rate that you use to pay down credit card balances with a high rate of interest—provided you pay off the loan as soon as possible and don't run up your credit cards again. In general, buying a home or refinancing to vastly reduce excessively high interest rates is usually good debt, as is generating limited debt to buy investments that are virtually guaranteed to meet expectations within a short period of time. (Note that stocks can be unexpectedly volatile and rarely justify a home equity loan.)

The only way credit card debt is not a bad debt is if you pay off your balance in full every month, prior to the grace period, so that you avoid paying any interest. Unfortunately, few of us are able to pay the balances in full each month, and all too often we overcharge, let our balances creep steadily upward, and end up paying the minimum amount due. And, since most credit cards carry exorbitant interest rates and slap us with high late fees and over-the-limit fees, using them for purchases typically generates bad debt. Plus, once you've racked up high-interest credit card debt, it's exceedingly hard and very, very costly to dig your way out.

Why We Have Become a Credit Card Nation

Statistics show that most Americans have increasingly used their credit cards to breach budget shortfalls or to buy things they cannot really afford. Some are literally staggering under the weight of exceptional credit card debt. Indeed, taken on a national basis, the amount of debt creates a bleak reality; taken on an individual basis, it can easily become catastrophic.

Knowledge is Power	Federal Reserve statistics reveal that the size of the total consumer debt grew nearly five times in size from 1980 ($355 billion) to 2001 ($1.7 trillion). Consumer debt in 2007 was $2.5 trillion. The average household in 2007 carried nearly $8,500 in credit card debt.

Fair Isaac Corporation, a company that helps the nation's largest banks and financial institutions assess credit risk, and is the developer of FICO scores and owner of FICO.com, analyzed a representative national sample of millions of consumer credit profiles to determine current credit card habits in America. The company deduced the following:

- On average, today's consumer has a total of thirteen credit obligations, including credit cards (department store charge cards, gas cards, or bank cards) and installment loans (auto loans, mortgage loans, student loans, and so on). Of these, nine are likely to be credit cards and four are likely to be installment loans.
- Less than half of all consumers have ever been reported as thirty or more days late on a payment; only three out of ten have been sixty or more days overdue; 77 percent have never had a loan or account ninety days overdue; and fewer than 20 percent have ever had a loan or account closed by the lender due to default.
- The typical consumer has access to approximately $19,000 on credit cards, but more than half are using less than 30 percent of their total credit card limit, which is considered very acceptable, dependent upon how many cards they have. Just over one in seven are using 80 percent or more of their credit card limit, which is alarmingly risky.
- The average consumer's oldest obligation is fourteen years old, indicating that he or she has been managing credit for some time.

- The average consumer has had only one inquiry on his or her accounts within the past year. Fewer than 6 percent had four or more inquiries resulting from a search for new credit. Excessive inquiries can be injurious to your credit rating.

This is *relatively* good news for America in terms of its citizens' financial solvency, but if you are one of the consumers who has maxed, or nearly maxed out, your credit cards, statistics won't alleviate your anxiety. If you are carrying credit card debt of $5,000 or more individually, or $10,000 or more as a family, given the high cost of interest and the high possibility of incurring additional charges, you may find that it takes a very long time to pay it off, or that you will have great difficulty paying it down to a more manageable level.

ONE-INCOME INQUIRY

How do I perform a credit ratio analysis?
Financial experts typically advise clients to ascertain their credit ratio analysis. You find this number by dividing your monthly income by your monthly expenses. A low ratio is 20 percent; a moderate ratio is 21–40 percent; and a high ratio is over 40 percent. If your ratio is moderate, it's time to pay down your debt, particularly credit card debt. If your ratio is high, you are in danger of becoming insolvent; that is, you cannot afford to incur additional debt and need to make paying down your debt a priority.

The Pros of Using Credit Cards

Before you think we completely denigrate credit cards, we'll mention a few pros to having them. Other than convenience, and perhaps minimal protection in case you need ready cash in an emergency situation, the biggest pro to having credit cards is that successful management of three bank cards and two department store accounts can, indeed, bolster your credit rating, allowing consumers to acquire loans if they really need them. However, lenders blanch when they see excessive credit cards, excessive applications for credit cards, excessive transferring of balances to new credit cards, maximization of credit limits, slow payments, late payments, chronic delinquencies, or other worrisome debt repayment habits.

Knowledge
is Power

◀ Americans both love and abuse their credit cards. Reportedly, the amount of outstanding personal credit card debt more than tripled between 1990 and 2002, from $173 billion to a whopping $661 billion.

The Cons of Using Credit Cards

The cons of credit cards frequently far outweigh the pros. Credit card issuers are constantly seeking customers who charge beyond their means and make minimum payments carrying 18 to 30 percent interest for long periods of time. Often the interest charges will double, or even triple, the amount originally charged, making you poor and the credit card company rich. Always keep in mind that credit card issuers make their money on interest and additional fees. Most credit cards now charge $29 to $39 in late charges, or for going over your credit limit, and both offenses may boost your interest rate. Using data from a cross section of major and minor card issuers, IndexCreditCards.com found that late and over-the-limit fees ranged from $0 to $39. However, most nationwide issuers charged between $29 and $39 in both categories. Your credit problems create the companies' profitability.

Knowledge
is Power

◀ If you charged $3,000 on your credit card with an APR of 17.12 percent and made minimum payments of $148.50 over the next two years, you would pay an extra $559, adding 18.6 percent to the total cost. With one late fee, your interest and fees could leap to 28 percent, raising your required monthly minimum to $159, and increasing the extra costs to $691, adding 23 percent to the total cost.

When you apply for a loan or seek a new credit card, potential lenders will acquire your credit report and review your debt-to-income ratio. If you have used well beyond 30 percent of the available credit on your credit cards, they may charge you high interest rates, decline your loan, or refuse additional credit.

Even when you have racked up large balances, credit card companies continue to barrage you with offers, and they all sound tempting, particularly when they offer a low-interest introductory rate. However, be aware that all credit card companies source your credit rating to determine your creditworthiness, and these inquiries may hurt your credit score in the long run. Also, those fabulous offers almost always come with caveats:

- The rate can triple within months.
- They will raise your rates if you miss one payment.
- They keep raising your credit limit and urging you to spend more money.

You have to read the small print—word for word—and monitor all of your statements to watch for hidden charges or elevations in your interest rate.

Avoid Department Store Credit Cards

Department and specialty stores are always trying to entice you to open an account. The sales clerks are trained to push these offers, which usually include 10 to 20 percent off your current purchase. They make it easy to sign on, but as soon as you do you are subject to dramatic interest rate increases. Department stores are notorious for charging high interest rates on their credit cards. Also, to open the account, they query the credit bureaus, and if you close the account soon afterward, both of these actions can negatively impact your credit rating. In 90 percent of the cases, it's not worth the extra 10 to 20 percent savings. Plus, an excess of department store credit cards on your credit report may diminish your creditworthiness and make it impossible for you to acquire a loan when you really need one to cover home repairs or medical emergencies.

ONE-INCOME INQUIRY

How will new credit card laws benefit consumers?
In 1996, the U.S. Supreme Court lifted restrictions on credit card companies, allowing them to charge you whatever they want for a late fee. Also, if you default on any credit account, universal default now permits any credit card company to brand you a high risk and raise your interest rates accordingly.

New regulations have recently been passed that offer improved protection for consumers from some of these abusive credit card lending practices, but these regulations don't go into effect until July 1, 2010. These new rules will:

- Stop credit card companies from raising interest rates on funds already borrowed unless those funds were borrowed on a card with a variable rate, or the minimum payment was late by more than thirty days.
- Prohibit credit card companies from levying a late fee if the bill was mailed to the consumer fewer than twenty-one days prior to the due date.
- Require payments to be applied in a fair way across credit card balances with different interest rates. This usually happens when your card balance is a mix of purchases made during a 0 percent or other promotional period, or if some of the balance is from a cash advance. With the new regulations, the payments must be applied to the highest interest balance.
- Prohibit credit card companies from charging interest on amounts already paid, through two-cycle billing. With two-cycle billing, the credit card company uses two months to calculate the average daily balance, which creates a distinct advantage for them.
- Restrict the financing of fees on credit cards so that the fees or deposits use up the majority of the available credit on the account.

Only opt to hold credit cards at stores you frequent often, and limit your choices to two or three at most. Then, keep those balances under 30 percent of available credit limits, and pay them off as soon as possible. Generally, when it comes to department store cards, if you cannot pay cash or use your debit card, you're better off paying with a bank credit card. Reduce your spending and protect your credit rating by just saying "no" to any and all new department or specialty store offers.

Create a Game Plan to Reduce Debt

Transferring balances to another card and opening new cards gives you the very false illusion that you can get your debt under control. This is a very bad idea. There is no way to address the problem but to tackle it head on and to cease all credit card spending. In the past, you could declare bankruptcy, wipe the slate relatively clean (never 100 percent), and rebuild your credit score over the course of seven years. However, bankruptcy laws have been recently rewritten, which means most people have only limited options to make debt go away. Many more people will have to face the consequences of a series of bad decisions made over the course of many years, and you do not want to find yourself in that position.

Create Debt Assessment Tables

The first thing you have to do is really assess your situation. You cannot tackle your debt unless and until you are ready to make a completely honest appraisal. You need to pull out all your credit card statements; education, car, home, and home equity loan statements; utility bills; insurance bills; and anything else that documents how much you owe. It's time to record the cold, hard reality of each. As you record them, rank them according to the urgency of payment. For example, your mortgage(s) and your car payment(s) would be at the top, while a credit card with the lowest balance would be at the bottom. Following is a sample table to help you start the process of tracking your debts.

CREDIT ASSESSMENT							
Creditor	Amount Owed	Minimum Payment	Interest Rate	Credit Limit	Due Date	What I Can Pay	Late Fees
First Home	$45,000	$500	7.95%	n/a	2nd	$500	$45
College Loan	$750	$89	6.7%	n/a	15th	$89	$27
Bank of America	$6,200	$120	18.95%	$8,000	25th	$120	$29
Macy's	$859	$45	24%	$900	16th	$45	$19

Read the Fine Print

Compiling the list of accounts also means that it's time for you to get out a magnifying glass and read the fine print. You're looking for the following:

- **Interest rate:** This is the annual percentage rate (APR) you pay for the privilege of using the credit card. Even if you opened the card at 9 percent, if you missed any payments, racked up one or more late payments, or surpassed your credit limit, the issuer may have added a stiff interest hike (unannounced, until July 2010, as noted above). Make sure you monitor your APR and ask for a reduction in rates if it spikes.
- **Periodic rate:** This is the interest rate you are charged on your purchases or balance each month. Divide your APR by twelve (months) to find your current periodic rate.
- **Finance charge:** This is the monthly fee added to your balance based on the monthly interest rate. Again, divide your APR by twelve and multiply that number by your balance to find your current finance charge.
- **Grace period:** This is the amount of time (twenty-five to twenty-eight days—or less!) that elapses between the purchase date and the date by which you can pay for the purchase and

avoid interest charges. If you are only making minimum payments on existing balances, you lose the advantage of paying within the grace period. Some cards no longer have grace periods, but they can be useful, so opt for cards that still offer them.

- **Fixed versus variable rate:** Most credit cards have variable rates, and the right to raise your rates at any time, for any reason (until July 2010, as noted above). Monitor this rate so that you can catch hikes in time to minimize damage.
- **Annual fees:** This can include a $40 to $80 fee for the privilege of using the card. Try to find a card that doesn't charge an annual fee—easiest to do when you have good credit. If you need to establish credit and paying an annual fee is the best you can do, go with it, but switch to a non-fee card as soon as possible.
- **Extra fees:** Additional charges can include balance transfer fees, cash advance fees, special services, and over-the-limit fees, all of which have risen in recent years and can be excessive.
- **Credit limit:** Ideally you want to whittle down your balance so that 70 percent of your credit limit is available—and then do whatever you can to keep it at that level.
- **Consequences:** If you don't pay the bill on time, will you lose your house, your car, or your account? How much will your interest rates increase if you go over your credit limit, are slow to pay, miss one month, pay less than the minimum, or fail to pay?

This information will help you know what needs to be paid first and construct a viable game plan for paying down your debt. If you are carrying substantial credit card debt, create a table that reflects this information for each of your credit cards. That way, you'll be able to pinpoint the problem cards and target them first. Once you've done these exercises, you'll be well on your way to conquering your debt. Congratulations! Knowledge is always better than denial, and you've just learned and taken some important steps in mastering your debt and becoming a savvy consumer.

Call Your Creditors to Ask for Assistance

Once you have your credit card accounts in order, it's time to call each credit card company (or department store) and request a reduction in your interest rate. If you have been a long-term, responsible customer with a good track record, you have leverage in asking them to accommodate your request, and some will actually comply fairly quickly. However, if the first person you speak with says that they are not authorized to lower the rate, ask to speak to a supervisor. You'll achieve the best results if you always maintain a professional, polite tone and calmly ask for what you want. If the first-level supervisor says they cannot accommodate you, ask to go another step up the ladder. Persist, and you will often succeed.

If you are going through a rough patch financially that you expect to smooth out, don't be afraid to share this information and to ask the supervisor if she will allow you to make interest-only payments for six months, or if she will assist you in setting up a long-term payment plan. The issuer may opt to freeze your account for the time being, but view this as a positive action, one that will help you get your finances back in line. Keep in mind that you can reopen your account when times are better.

Institute a Plan to Pay Down Your Debt

Okay, now it's time to create an action plan to pay down your debt. Using the assessment tables that you created earlier, rate the urgency of each account. For example, house payments, car payments, and furniture payments always take priority over credit card debt. Now, add up the amounts in the minimum payment column and compute your budgeted living expenses (these will include car maintenance, transportation costs, and groceries, for example), and deduct both of these totals from your net, or take-home, income. What's left is the amount of money you can use to pay down your credit card debt.

Generally, you'll want to pay down the cards with the highest rate of interest first. However, if all of your cards are maxed out, and all the interest rates are in the same range, you may want to distribute funds to bring them all down to a more manageable balance. If one or two cost significantly more to carry, make minimum payments on everything else and distribute the remaining funds to those two cards. If you have too many cards, consider canceling the ones with the highest interest rate after you finish paying the balance. Once you have paid off a creditor, use the funds that you had been using to pay down the next costliest card.

ONE-INCOME INQUIRY

What are my rights when it comes to paying down debt?
If a collection agency is hounding you, you do have certain rights under the Fair Debt Collection Practices Act (FDCPA), as follows:

- If you ask them to stop calling, they cannot continue to call unless they are calling to say they are stopping all efforts to collect, or that they are suing you. Always send a follow-up letter to the agency to verify your request, noting your rights under the FDCPA.
- Even if they threaten to sue you or to garnish your wages if you don't agree to a repayment plan or settlement, they cannot sue you or garnish your wages without a court settlement. Their only recourse is to return the debt to the original creditor, or that creditor's attorney.
- They cannot threaten violence or use obscene language.
- If you request that they not call because you cannot take personal calls at work, they cannot call you at work, and they can call only between 8 a.m. and 9 p.m. at your home.
- They cannot send mail with visible indication of attempted collection.

If you have difficulty finding funds to pay down your debt, call the creditors one by one and alert them to your situation. Ask them if they will agree to a repayment plan that you can afford. Utility companies often have plans in place that will spread out your payments, or they'll offer reduced payments. Credit card companies would rather work with you than lose you as a customer, and it's worth the effort to ask them to work with you on a plan to pay off the account. They will likely freeze your account, but they may also freeze additional charges, and paying them directly is preferable to having them turn over the debt to a collection agency.

When you negotiate via telephone, always take notes, including the date, the name and title of the person you spoke with, what was agreed upon, and any other pertinent information, and then follow up with a letter stating the same information. If your creditor agrees to accept a lower amount as total repayment, make sure you have a letter verifying this information in hand before you send a check.

Debt Management Programs

If you are mired in credit debt and unable to find sufficient funds to pay down credit cards, you may want to consider a credit counseling or debt management program (DMP). Basically, you meet with a counselor who helps you ascertain how much you can afford to pay your creditors each month. The counselor negotiates with your creditors on your behalf to achieve lower interest rates and lowered, or frozen, fees in exchange for a repayment plan. Then, you pay the agency a set amount per month that it distributes to your creditors. While this may sound ideal, there are both pros and cons to seeking the services of debt management programs to repay your debt.

The Pros of Debt Management Programs

Credit card debt statistics are fairly hard to find because these statistics are not routinely gathered on a national basis, nor are they part of a standard database that is open to the general public. However, according to a 2002 study done by the Credit Research Center at Georgetown University in concert with the National Foundation for

Credit Counseling (published by Money-zine.com), approximately 2 million to 2.5 million Americans seek the help of a credit counselor each year, mostly to avoid bankruptcy, and mostly as the result of financial difficulties due to job loss, an interruption to their income due to illness, or a divorce or separation.

Knowledge is Power

Current statistics on debt gathered by the U.S. Federal Reserve reveal the following:

- Consumer debt in 2008 stood at $2.6 trillion.
- In 2008, the average household carried nearly $8,700 in credit card debt.
- As of the twelve months ending June 2006, there were 1.5 million consumer bankruptcy filings, including 1.1 million Chapter 7 filings, 0.1 million filings for Chapter 11, and 0.3 million Chapter 13 bankruptcies.

If you're at this stage, you can take heart in knowing that you're not alone. And the real benefit to working with a credit counselor to repay your debt is that it can save you from falling farther behind or even from the brink of bankruptcy—a far worse fate.

It is, however, vitally important that you do some preliminary research to make sure you find a reputable agency. Contact the National Foundation for Consumer Credit (NFCC) at *www.nfcc.org* for information specific to credit management. You can also call your local Better Business Bureau or chamber of commerce to find out whether a specific agency has complaints lodged against it.

The Cons of Debt Management Programs

The only real con to debt management programs is that most will report the DMP to the credit reporting agencies, meaning it will show up on your credit history. If you have substantial debt, the benefit may outweigh the risk, but ask your counselor if reporting can be avoided. Even if it cannot be avoided, the presence of a DMP on your credit report is not as detrimental as a bankruptcy, and shows your intention to repay all of your debt. There's something to be said for honorably and responsibly discharging debt, and eventually you should be able to restore your credit rating. Although it's generally reported that bankruptcies are removed from your credit history in seven to ten years, they can, in fact, remain on your extended credit history for the rest of your life. A wise consumer would opt for a DMP long before bankruptcy loomed large on the horizon.

What Should I Look for in a Debt Management Company?

Look for a company that tailors a solution to address *your* problems, rather than one that steers you to the easiest or most profitable solution—one that would benefit only the agency and the creditors.

ONE-INCOME INQUIRY

What should I avoid when choosing a debt management company?
It's best to avoid choosing a debt management company that has or does any of the following:

- They have multiple unresolved complaints with the Better Business Bureau.
- They advise you to stop paying your creditors.
- They charge excessive fees.
- They do not require a written agreement with you.
- They promise to remove or change negative information from your credit history.

Ask about fees upfront. Often you can find free or very low cost counseling and debt management programs. Look for nonprofit agencies, or for highly reputable agencies with reasonable fees—less than $75 for an initial interview and a monthly rate between $15 and $35.

Also, shop around for an accredited agency that has trained and certified counselors and will offer debt management training programs to help you establish healthy financial habits. If you feel strong-armed, or unheard, you are probably being sold services you don't need. Trust your instincts. Your credit history is an asset you need to protect.

Avoid "High-Risk" Borrowing to Pay Down Debts

In desperation, you may consider taking out a loan to achieve debt consolidation, but in general this is not a productive path. Far too often, you end up with all your debt bundled into one huge loan, with a very high interest rate and excessive fees, and the ability to charge up your credit cards again. You've all seen the commercials on television suggesting that it's easy for anyone who suffers a calamity to call a phone number to acquire a quick $10,000 to cover her escalating bills. Unfortunately, these "high-risk" lenders are bad news. There are three very important reasons to avoid high-risk borrowing for debt consolidation:

1. They have you over a barrel, and they determine the terms: variable rates versus fixed rates, late fees, minimum payments, and so on.
2. They charge exorbitant interest rates. You'll rack up interest charges that will quickly double or even triple your debt.
3. They frequently charge hefty upfront fees.

Of course, the worst aspect is that, all too often, the consumer then charges up his or her credit cards again, creating a financial disaster.

You also want to steer clear of direct-mail offers to consolidate your debt or to clear up your credit reports. First, any company sending mailers is likely to charge very high fees. Second, these companies do not have an inside track or a magic wand, and they have absolutely zero ability to discharge legitimate debt. Clearing up your credit reports is a task you can and should handle on your own.

Should I Settle Old Accounts?

If you have a long-standing unpaid bill and are applying for home financing, you may want to offer a settlement in return for a clean slate. Creditors often leap at offers to pay half of the original amount, particularly if it's been hanging out there a long time. If you do this, however, it is VITALLY important that you request a letter from the creditor agreeing to the terms of the settlement in return for wiping the slate clean. Don't pay them until you have a written record that they are accepting this payment as final payment on monies due. You want them to report that you are "paying the account in full." If they fail to clear your credit report, you will need this letter to clear it.

Also, if you have a lot of old debts that you need to clear, it may be wise to hire a lawyer to negotiate repayment. In some cases, the old debts may "disappear" seven years after the last payment, and inquiries may "reopen" them. Lawyers will know how to negotiate settlements without stirring up the dust, which could save you hundreds, or thousands, of dollars and prevent negative items from reappearing.

Develop a Cash Mentality

Now that you know the difference between good and bad debt, and you've been warned about incurring further credit card debt and been given concrete suggestions about paying down your debt, you are on the path to becoming a much savvier consumer. Hereafter, any time you are tempted to whip out a credit card to purchase something that will not increase in value, do yourself a big favor: Ask yourself if you could pay cash. If you can't afford to pay for it with cash, you're better off not buying it. This way, you'll soon become familiar with exactly how much expendable income you have per month, and the likelihood that you'll overspend decreases.

Ideally, it's best to truly use your credit cards sparingly—almost strictly as an emergency safety net. If you're using your credit cards and paying off the balances in full, then fine. But if you are racking up credit charges, maxing out your cards, and paying minimum balances, you are endangering your long-term stability and decreasing your ability to obtain low-interest loans. It's vitally important that you reduce any bad debt that is dragging you down. When things are back in line, keep in mind that good debt creates wealth, while bad debt severely decreases your chance of ever being wealthy—or even solvent.

To make sure you're doing everything you can to control your debt, ask yourself:

❑ Have I created a thorough assessment of my debt?
❑ Have I created and instituted a system for paying off high-interest debt?
❑ Have I called my credit card companies to ask for lower interest rates?
❑ Have I limited my credit to three credit cards, a gas card, and one department store card?
❑ Am I paying all my bills on time?
❑ Am I paying more than the minimum amount due?
❑ Am I keeping my debt at 30 percent of my available credit?
❑ Am I paying down my credit cards regularly?
❑ Am I avoiding late fees?
❑ Am I checking my credit scores annually?
❑ Am I doing everything possible to increase my credit score?

Making Housing Decisions

Chapter Six

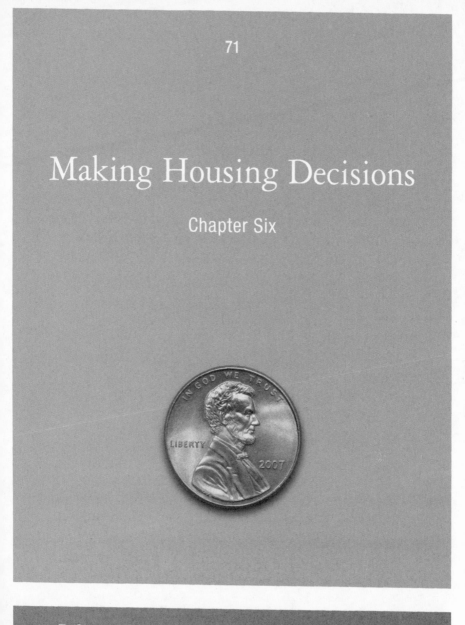

To Stay or Not to Stay in Your Home • What Are the Benefits of Owning Your Home? • What You Can Afford • Should You Apply for a Home Equity Loan? • Should You Refinance? • What You Need to Know Before You Sign • Why It's Not Always Smart to Own • The Benefits of Downsizing

IF YOU ARE suddenly thrust into a one-income status, you may find yourself in a tight economic bind. For some families this may mean surrendering their current home or acquiring an equity loan to tide them over.

To Stay or Not to Stay in Your Home

One primary question you will face will be whether or not you can continue to live in your current home. Whether you own or rent, you'll have to carefully assess how much you can afford to pay for housing. If you own a house, those costs include not only the mortgage but also related expenses, such as property taxes, upkeep, and insurance.

There are several questions you need to answer:

- How much will your current mortgage and upkeep, or rent payments, strain your budget?
- Can you stay in the house and save for retirement and college?
- How much equity do you have in the house?
- Is the real estate market healthy or in a slump?
- Do you have relatives who might want to invest in your house?

If you can afford to stay in your current home, and still have enough money to build an emergency fund and save for your retirement, doing so may be your ideal situation.

Real estate markets have recurring cycles. If the real estate market is strong, the likelihood is greater that sellers would at least make a small profit if they had to sell their house. This likelihood increases with the number of years that you have owned the property.

Unfortunately, you have no control over the vicissitudes of the real estate market, but you can take heart in knowing that the markets both surge and then self-correct by slowing or edging backward. If you can afford to remain in your house, you have the luxury of waiting for an uptrend.

What Are the Benefits of Owning Your Home?

Owning your home offers many benefits; chief among them is that your home is typically your primary and largest investment, and an investment in real estate is usually the most profitable and secure investment you can make. Even though the real estate market may experience downturns, over the long haul your home is likely to increase substantially in value, providing a hedge against inflation. Also, as you pay the mortgage each month, your equity or ownership builds (unless you have an interest-only loan), and the amount of interest you pay on your home loan can provide a substantial tax deduction each year. In contrast, renting doesn't build equity for you and doesn't provide any tax deductions.

Knowledge is Power ◄ Through the tax breaks offered, which are based on tax bracket percentages and your monthly mortgage, the government basically subsidizes homeowners. Why? Homeowners tend to stay in their jobs longer, work harder, and support the economy. It's good for the overall economy and helps keep communities clean, safe, and stable.

Of course, owning your home—as long as you can comfortably afford the monthly mortgage payments—also provides maximum stability for your family. Let's review the financial benefits of owning your home.

Homes Usually Appreciate in Value

Despite occasional downturns, usually in reaction to a bubble in which housing prices soared—as we have recently experienced—single-family homes have consistently appreciated, or gained in value. For greater appreciation, maintain your home as best you can, and invest in renovations that increase its value, such as remodeling bathrooms or kitchens or improving the landscaping.

You Can Deduct Interest Payments

Since mortgage interest is fully tax-deductible—as long as your mortgage balance is less than the price you paid for your home—home ownership provides a superb tax shelter. This is particularly true in the early years of home ownership, when the bulk of your monthly mortgage payment is allocated to the interest you will pay over the life of the loan rather than to amount you pay toward the principal, or original price of the home.

Your Home Qualifies for Capital Gains Exclusions

As long as you have lived in your home for two of the five years prior to selling it, you can exclude up to $250,000 for an individual ($500,000 for a married couple) of the profit earned from capital gains taxes. In the past, you had to buy a replacement home or move up the ladder, unless you were over age fifty-five, but this is no longer true. Anyone can exclude these thresholds from capital gains taxes every twenty-four months, which means you could sell every two years and pocket your profit—subject to limitation—free from taxation.

Mortgage Reduction Builds Equity

Each month that you own the home, part of your monthly payment amortizes—or is applied to the principal balance of your loan—which reduces your obligation, or the amount you owe. This is the way amortization works: The principal portion of your combined principal and interest payment increases slightly every month. Interest then is calculated on the declining principal balance, which means that each month, more of your payment goes toward principal and less goes toward interest. The amount of principal paid is lowest on your first mortgage payment and highest on your last. If you have owned your home for ten years or more, you may have whittled down the principal enough to have earned substantial equity in your home, and with each payment you will be paying more principal than will someone who has owned their home for only one or two years.

What You Can Afford

According to Elizabeth Warren, coauthor of *The Two-Income Trap: Why Middle-Class Mothers & Fathers Are Going Broke*, "A family that doesn't have the financial resources to put together a down payment on their own, is fifteen to twenty times more likely to lose the home on foreclosure." It boils down to this: If you haven't been able to save up some money for a down payment, it's a clear sign that your income is too erratic or your expenses are already too high, and that you can't afford to buy a house right now.

"A big part of the two-income trap is that families have basically bid up the cost of living. A generation ago, an average family could buy an average home on one income. Today you can't do that in three-quarters of American cities," Warren explains. "We all know that housing prices are going up, but what most people don't realize is that this has become a family problem. Up until recently, when housing values have been falling in many areas of the country, housing prices traditionally rose twice as fast for families with kids."

Knowledge is Power ◄ Amelia Warren Tyagi, coauthor of *The Two-Income Trap: Why Middle-Class Mothers & Fathers Are Going Broke*, states, [In 2004] "Average mortgage expenses have gone up seventy times faster than the average father's income, and the only way families are keeping up is by bringing in two incomes . . . [single-income families] are five times more likely to go bankrupt, and three times more likely to lose their homes [than double-income families]. Families are going broke on the basics—housing, health insurance, and education."

Most home lenders base their decision on how much you can afford to pay for a house by computing your gross monthly income. Lenders typically suggest that you allocate 25 to 35 percent of your gross monthly income as an acceptable housing expense—whether it's rent or a mortgage. Staying around 28 percent is advisable. To verify that you are responsibly assessing mortgage affordability, lenders will usually also ask for a complete accounting on your monthly long-term debt payments (anything that will require a minimum of ten months to pay). If your earnings potential is likely to increase, or if you have a long history of stellar credit, a lender may offer you more leeway. However, if your long-term debt payments combined with the proposed house payment is more than 36 percent of your gross monthly income, lenders will likely deny your loan. Also, your gross monthly income is not always a good barometer, as payroll deductions can make a huge impact on your real take-home pay.

To figure out what you can truly afford, refer to Chapter 4. Also, if you have not already done so, follow the necessary steps to compile your balance sheet and your monthly budget. This process will give you very accurate, realistic numbers.

Also keep in mind that additional housing expenses, such as insurance, property taxes, and upkeep, can add a significant amount to your monthly debt column. Make sure you compute these costs and add them to the monthly mortgage payments in determining your monthly housing expense.

Should You Apply for a Home Equity Loan?

A home equity loan is similar to any other type of secured loan that you might get from your bank or credit union, with one major exception: Home equity loans are essentially a second mortgage. You borrow a lump sum of money and then pay it back in monthly installments over a finite period of time, such as ten to fifteen years.

Generally, you lock in an interest rate at the time you borrow the money. Yes, the interest, or a portion of the interest, is usually deductible on your taxes, and the rate may be far lower than what you're paying for credit card debt, but if you default on a home equity loan, the lender can take your home.

There are two types of home equity loans: the standard home equity loan (HEL) and the home equity line of credit (HELOC). The standard home equity loan secures one lump sum for which the borrower pays a set monthly amount. HELOC secures approval for a certain loan amount and allows you to choose when and how much you access, up to the approved limit. It equates to a checkbook or credit card issued with a set, approved amount in the account. You can choose when and how much you withdraw, and payments will commence based on the amount and interest owed. Generally you don't pay anything if you don't use the money, unless your line of credit requires an annual fee.

The Pros of Home Equity Loans

The pros for a home equity loan need to be carefully weighed against the cons. The pros are as follows:

- Interest rates are generally lower than credit card or unsecured loans.
- You can use the loan amount however you wish. Ideally, this would be to pay down higher-interest debt; to pay for an unexpected, expensive home repair; or to fund an emergency.
- Interest on loan amounts up to $100,000 may be tax-deductible. This tax-deductible portion is based on a percentage, so if you're in a higher income bracket it may not apply.
- Having a HELOC can function as a short-term emergency fund, as long as you use it only when absolutely necessary and you can pay it back within a short period of time.

Your first consideration should be whether it's necessary, and whether you can easily afford the monthly payment. If you can, and if the reason you need the money has long-term benefits, it may make real sense to apply for a HEL; however, limit the amount you borrow to what's necessary. In other words, don't decide that you may as well borrow an extra $3,000 to save in case you need it. Chances are that money would be spent on trifles before you blink.

ONE-INCOME INQUIRY

Are interest deductions on Home Equity Loans tax deductable?

Yes, but the interest deductions on a HEL or HELOC are not a dollar-for-dollar reduction of your taxes, just a percentage; and with tax rates declining, the deduction may not be as valuable as you think. For example, if your mortgage interest deduction is $15,000 and your marginal tax rate is 15 percent, the reduction in tax would be $2,250. Plus, if your adjusted gross income is high, the phase-out for itemized deductions may kick in, preventing you from taking a full deduction, if any at all. Research the benefits before making your decision.

If you want to open a HELOC to use as an emergency fund, it will be important to really adhere to that intended purpose: don't withdraw any money you don't really need. Otherwise, you can run up to your limit without even realizing how much you tapped. If you open the line of credit, you may want to lock the checkbook in a safe-deposit box or at least under lock and key at home so that you'll always have time to ruminate carefully, and discuss any planned withdrawals with your partner.

The Cons of Home Equity Loans

The cons to having a HEL or HELOC are as follows:

- For a HEL or a HELOC, you use your home as collateral. If your income drops and you cannot make the payments, your home will be at risk. In contrast, credit card debt is unsecured;

if necessary, you can suspend payment without losing your house.

- If real estate values drop, you may end owing more than your home is worth.
- You may lock in a rate and then see rates drop 2 to 3 percent. Or, the interest rate you pay on your HELOC (typically those rates are at least 1 percent above prime) could rise and require larger payments. The Prime Rate is the interest rate charged by major banks on loans to the largest and highest-rated customers. Consumer rates begin at prime and go upward dependent upon many factors.
- Some lenders require a minimum withdrawal from HELOC accounts, which means you may only need $600, but have to withdraw $1,500. Read your contract carefully.
- Because your HEL or HELOC will likely be $15,000 or more, while your maximum credit card debt may total $10,000, it will likely take you longer to pay off a HEL or HELOC, which means the debt may cost you more in the long run.

Using a home equity loan as an ATM or credit card can be extremely risky, particularly when relying on one income. It's one thing to apply for a home equity loan to cover an extraordinary and unavoidable expense, or even to use it once to consolidate excessive, high-interest credit card debt, but using it for anything other than extraordinary expenses only compounds your debt. Among the worst things you can do is take out a home equity loan to pay off your credit cards, and then charge up your credit cards again. Always be very aware that using a home equity loan increases the amount you owe on your home, and that an inability to meet those payments could quickly lead to foreclosure.

If you are dependent upon one income, make sure you can cover the payments if the wage earner becomes ill or gets laid off. Most important, don't think of home equity loans as "quick fixes." Deciding whether or not to use your home as collateral for another loan is an extremely important decision for your financial future.

Are Home Equity Loans Right for Me?

When deciding whether or not to acquire or access a HEL, it's important to consider long-term versus short-term gains. If you need the loan to make necessary repairs, it may make sense in the long term to borrow the amount needed. Upgrading to a better car or taking the whole family to Disneyland for a week are short-term goals and not a prudent way to use funds acquired from a HEL. However, borrowing one set amount and using it to fund something that will provide long-term value—such as a renovation or trading your credit card debt at 22 percent interest for a HEL at 8.5 percent—may make sense. When making this decision, keep in mind that while your creditors can harass you if you default on credit card payments, they cannot take away your home, as the home equity lender can—and will, if you default for an extended period of time.

Don't be swayed by the fact that you can usually use the interest paid on a HEL as a deduction on your tax return. Unless you have a high income, those deductions may not save you any real money.

Knowledge is Power	According to the Consumer Bankers Association (CBA), the average HEL is $33,000, and the average HELOC is $58,800. The average outstanding balance on a HELOC is $28,500.

There are times when opening a HELOC might make sense. These include times when:

- You need to make renovations to your home and will be paying for these repairs over a long period of time.
- You don't have an emergency fund, but you have the wisdom of Job when deciding when to access the funds and the discipline to pay the loan off quickly.

- You have already paid off your first mortgage and only plan to use the account sparingly for essential reasons—such as renovations to boost your home's value, or for medical expenses.
- You are approaching retirement and because your level of income will fall substantially, you may not be able to qualify for a HELOC after you retire. Again, this makes sense only if you don't use the funds unless absolutely necessary.

Times when acquiring a HEL or HELOC makes no sense at all include when:

- You are having difficulty making your monthly mortgage payments.
- You have a variable interest rate or a large balloon payment on the horizon.
- You already have zero equity or a negative amortization loan.
- You're maxing out the value of your house and may have to move or put your home up for lease within a year.
- You're a young homeowner who isn't on strong financial legs and has limited experience managing a monthly budget.
- You are approaching retirement and owe very little on your house. Why bump up the monthly payment if there is any way to avoid it?
- You can find less expensive ways to borrow, such as buying a car when the dealers offer 0 percent financing, or when you can refinance and secure a lower fixed rate over a 15- to 30-year period.
- You're borrowing money to help pay for all those years you lived above your means by racking up credit card debt. If you haven't taken steps to rein in your spending, don't put your home at risk!

If these scenarios sound familiar, rather than opting for a HEL or HELOC, you may want to consider refinancing.

Should You Refinance?

Refinancing may be beneficial if:

- You can secure a lower interest rate. If your interest rate is significantly higher than current rates, and you qualify for the lowest rates, a refinance may make perfect sense. It can be a good idea to refinance if the interest rate is 1.5 to 2 percent less than your current rate.
- You have an adjustable-rate mortgage (ARM) and want the security of a fixed rate.
- You have a jumbo loan. Rates on jumbo mortgages run about three-eighths of a percent higher than normal rates, so it can pay to refinance when you reach the cutoff for a so-called conforming loan. The limit for conforming mortgages was $625,500 as of January 1, 2009.
- You want to escalate payments to lower interest. Low-rate periods provide a window for borrowers to shorten their loan terms from a 30-year to a 15-year mortgage, saving significant interest payments. If you can afford it, this will save money over the long run.
- You're paying for private mortgage insurance (PMI). If you didn't have 20 percent for a down payment, or if the equity in your home is less than 20 percent of the original purchase price, you are probably paying between $35 and $150 a month for PMI. Refinancing would allow you to clear the requirement.
- You have other high-rate debt. Mortgage debt often provides the lowest rates available, and the interest is tax-deductible. So if you have untapped equity in your home, you may want to opt for a cash-out refinance. This would increase your mortgage, but allow you to pay off higher-rate loans.

Before leaping to your telephone, use online calculators to see how much you'll save by refinancing. Here are a few popular ones:

- *www.lendingtree.com/smartborrower/Calculators/Mortgage-Calculators .aspx*
- *www.mortgage-calc.com*
- *www.bankrate.com/brm/mortgage-calculator.asp*

Even if you spend time researching the lowest rates, always query your lender first, as they may be willing to lower your rate without going through the normal paperwork gymnastics. Also, keep in mind that you will likely pay additional loan fees, including an assessment if you have owned the house for a long time.

ONE-INCOME INQUIRY

What are the warning signs that a lender may be disreputable?

If you are ready to acquire a HEL or HELOC, signs that the lender may be disreputable include the following:

- They tell you it's okay to "slightly exaggerate" your income or falsify information on the loan application. Never do this! It's illegal.
- They urge you to apply for more money than you need, or for a loan with higher monthly payments than you can afford. They are trying to bolster their commission with no concern for what happens to you.
- They change the terms you discussed. They know most people don't read the fine print.
- They ask you to sign blank forms. Never do this! Draw a line through all blank spots and initial them.
- They pressure you to sign "today." High pressure is never a good sign. Deals don't expire overnight.

Note: Lists of government agencies that can help you find reputable lenders can be found in Appendix C, under Consumer Loan Information.

What You Need to Know Before You Sign

Before you refinance or take out a HEL or HELOC, it's very important that you understand exactly what you are undertaking. The best way to do this is to make sure you ask the lender, broker, or representative the following questions:

- Is this a loan or a line of credit? Make sure it's what you want.
- What are the monthly payments? Make sure you can afford them.
- What is the annual percentage rate (APR) on the loan? The APR is the cost of credit, expressed as a yearly rate; use it to compare loans.
- Will the interest rate be fixed or variable? If variable, when and by how much will it increase?
- Is there a balloon payment: a large single payment after a series of low monthly payments?
- How many years will you have to repay the loan?
- How much are late or missed payment penalties?
- Is there a prepayment penalty?
- Are there points or fees involved? One point equals 1 percent of the loan amount. Generally, the higher the points, the lower the interest rate. Traditional financial institutions normally charge between 1 and 3 percent of the loan amount in points and fees.
- Are the application fees refundable if you don't get the loan?
- Are there any closing costs, such as the broker's commission?
- Does the loan package include optional credit insurance, which pays if you become disabled and cannot make your payments? Don't buy insurance you don't need. If you want it, ask if you can pay for it on a monthly basis after the loan is approved and closed. Adding it in will be too expensive. With monthly payments, you usually don't pay interest and can cancel if necessary.

After you have answers to these questions, shop around and see how other loan agencies compare. It's a competitive business, so don't be afraid to make large lenders and independent brokers compete for your business. Tell them you are shopping for the best deal and ask if they can lower the points, fees, or interest rate. Then, make sure the lender you select is reputable. Once you're confident that you've selected the best lender, ask for the following:

- A "Good Faith Estimate" of all loan charges. Lenders are required to send this estimate within three days after you sign a loan application.
- Blank copies of the forms you'll sign at closing. When you get home, read them carefully, and if you don't understand something, ask for an explanation.
- Advance copies of the forms you'll sign at closing—with the terms filled in. Make sure the terms, conditions, rates, and other details have all remained the same. By law, you can inspect the final settlement statement (also called the HUD-1 or HUD-1A form) one day prior to closing. Again, review everything carefully to make sure nothing was changed.
- A copy of the documents you signed. Do this before you leave the closing.

ONE-INCOME INQUIRY

What if I change my mind?

When you use your home as security for a HEL (or for a second mortgage loan or a line of credit), federal law gives you three business days after signing the loan papers to cancel the deal. You don't need a reason, but you must cancel in writing. The lender is legally required to return any money you have paid to date.

Why It's Not Always Smart to Own

If you are already renting, or are finding that surrendering your house and renting is a more viable option, take heart. There are legitimate reasons for renting rather than owning a house. The detriments of home ownership include these:

- Late house payments seriously erode your credit rating
- If you default, you lose the house *and* your initial down payment
- You bear the cost of repairs and upkeep
- You pay rising real estate taxes and insurance
- You may have to borrow against your home to stay afloat, thereby diminishing or losing equity
- Housing prices may stay flat or decline, eroding equity
- If you sell, you have to pay the real estate agent's commission (typically 5–6 percent)

In contrast, there are benefits to renting:

- The landlord pays for all repairs and upkeep of the property
- The landlord pays property taxes and home insurance (you may want renter's insurance)
- You can free up the cash you would have spent on a down payment
- Flexibility: You can move faster and cheaper, if necessary
- You can try out a neighborhood to see if it's where you want to live long-term

Renting may be a better solution for you, at least temporarily. If your one-income situation is going to be relatively short-term, it may be to your advantage to do whatever you can to stay in your home. However, if your situation is long-term, you may want to weigh the benefits of selling your house and renting for a while, particularly if your mortgage puts a real strain on your monthly budget. There also are other options.

The Benefits of Downsizing

If you've decided that you cannot afford to remain in your house, downsizing may be a viable option and a solid investment decision.

Other than selling your current house to move into one that's smaller, perhaps in a less-expensive neighborhood, buying either a condominium or a cooperative could help you save a lot of money. The benefits of buying either a condo or a co-op include these:

- You still own real estate that can escalate in value
- You receive the tax advantages that come with ownership
- Your condo or co-op will likely accrue equity over time
- You may be able to secure an equity loan or equity line of credit
- You may be able to remain in your preferred neighborhood, schools, etc.
- In some cases, all you have to maintain is the interior of your home, as the monthly fee may provide for landscaping and exterior repairs

Buying a Condominium

Purchasing a condo or townhouse means that you buy an undivided interest in one unit in a group of units and share ownership in the common areas. You pay your own mortgage, plus an additional monthly fee allocated to maintenance. It is also important to note that condo fees are very likely to increase on an annual basis.

When purchasing a condo it is important to carefully review the following documents:

- **Bylaws.** Bylaws are basically communal rules. They authorize the governing board to assess fees, hire managers, and carry out other operational duties, such as repairs or landscaping decisions. Typically, each condo owner has voting power, but it's important to review the bylaws to get a realistic feel for how a particular condo organization functions.
- **House Rules.** These rules delineate what condo owners can and cannot do in the common areas, such as erect fences or storage sheds, alter the landscaping, park recreational vehicles, and so on.

- **Covenants, Conditions, and Restrictions (CCR).** CCRs are the nitty-gritty rules about how individual owners can use their property. Many condo organizations will require that the unit is owner-occupied; that is, no rentals. You want to make sure that you know the proportion of rentals in the condo organizations. For example, if there are an excessive number of rental units (30 to 50 percent), lenders may label the property "investment real estate," which could negatively affect your ability to secure a loan.
- **Purchase Agreement.** The purchase agreement provides the owner the right to fully inspect all documents pertinent to ownership. They often provide financing and inspection contingencies that will allow you to renege on your purchase agreement if you discover something that you cannot live with prior to closing.

Knowledge is Power

Both condos and co-ops usually have a resident-elected governing board of directors that oversees ongoing maintenance and makes the final decisions on repairs and rules. However, in most cases, each owner does have a voice and can vote on issues presented, including the timing or cost of repairs. Your vote may be weighted by the size of your condo or co-op.

Buying a Cooperative

Cooperatives, or co-ops, offer you an opportunity to buy shares in a cooperative that owns a property. Your share allows you exclusive use of a single-unit apartment. When buying a co-op, ask the following:

- What are the historical sales figures for the past few years? This will give you a concrete idea about the rising or falling value.
- What is the per-unit value of each unit in the communal mortgage and any variances? This will give you a more realistic idea of how much your unit is worth.

- What is the status of property taxes; that is, how much they are likely to rise?
- Are any major repairs on the horizon, and how will they be funded?
- Are there lawsuits pending against the cooperative?

When buying either a condo or co-op, you should ask for full disclosure on the reserve fund—historical and current. In most cases, a portion of your monthly assessment goes into a reserve fund to cover major repairs. Ideally, you will want to know how much is currently in the reserve fund, what percentage of your monthly fees go into the fund, and what repairs are planned for the next five to ten years. If the reserve fund is not adequate to cover repairs, the condo or the co-op may have the right to enact a "special assessment," which means they may demand additional funds to cover repairs. If the homeowners cannot pay the special assessment, the condo or co-op association may be able to place a lien on your property. If you aren't able to pay the special assessment or pay off the lien, that could lead to foreclosure.

Avoiding Foreclosure

Chapter Seven

The Rising Foreclosure Trend • Understand the Ramifications of Foreclosure • What to Do if Disaster Strikes • Negotiate with the Lender • Recent Changes That May Help • Last-Gasp Strategies • Be Wary of Foreclosure Rescue Scams • Tax Consequences of Debt Cancellation

ONE MAJOR CONSEQUENCE of economic instability is the loss of one's home to foreclosure—a forced sale at less than market value. As we have all been learning lately, foreclosures are a threat to our national economy, and a complete financial disaster for those who are forced to endure it.

The Rising Foreclosure Trend

When the Midyear 2007 U.S. Foreclosure Market Report was released by RealtyTrac, an online marketplace for foreclosure properties, it showed that foreclosure filings—default notices, auction sale notices, and bank repossessions—were up more than 30 percent from the previous six-month period, and up more than 55 percent from the first six months of 2006. The report also shows a foreclosure rate of one foreclosure filing for every 134 U.S. households for the first half of the year. In 2008, foreclosures continued rising at alarming rates, and many experts have predicted that trend to continue well into 2009.

ONE-INCOME INQUIRY

Will the government help?
If your interest rate has increased, making it increasingly difficult for you to meet your house payments, you may qualify for help under a federal plan known as FHA Secure, which insures loans for Americans who may have been late with a couple of payments and are facing interest rate resets. Under this program you may be able to lower your rates or extend your loan. The caveat is that you must be otherwise reliably creditworthy; that is, able to provide verifiable income, have a solid credit rating, and live in your home.

Foreclosures arise from many different circumstances, such as refinancing to acquire loans beyond the value of the property; having an adjustable rate mortgage that resets to a payment that the owner can't afford; having a balloon payment that the owner cannot meet; or having a 100 percent financed subprime mortgage in which the owner didn't save up for a down payment and has no equity. Often these owners have low credit scores or exceptional debt and find it easier to abandon the house than struggle to hold onto it.

Understand the Ramifications of Foreclosure

It is important to note that foreclosure proceedings vary from state to state and that the type of loan you have, whether a trust deed or a mortgage, can determine how long you may be able to remain in the home if you go into foreclosure. A trust deed transfers the title to the property to a trustee, often a title company that holds the title as security for a loan. When the loan is paid off, the title is transferred to the borrower. With a mortgage, the title to the property remains with the borrower, and the loan company has a recorded lien on the property. In states where mortgages are used, you may be allowed to remain in the house for almost a year, whereas in states where trust deeds are used, you may only have a four-month window before you are forced to vacate.

Knowledge is Power	Almost every state provides a period of redemption, which means that—for a certain length of time—you have an irrevocable right to prevent foreclosure by paying all foreclosure costs, back interest, and the missed principal payments. Make sure you know your rights. If you cannot afford to consult a real estate lawyer, log on to *www.hud.gov* or call (800) 569-4287. When you call, you will be offered an option to receive an automated referral to three local low-cost (or free) counseling agencies.

Usually, once a lender files a Notice of Default, it's too late to prevent foreclosure proceedings. Lenders file the Notice of Default to protect their interest in the property; it's up to you to take swift action to protect your interest. If you contact your lender when the problem first occurs, you may be able to negotiate a grace period.

Knowledge is Power	Stay in your home—you may not qualify for certain types of assistance if you move out. Renting your home changes it from a primary residence to an investment property, which may leave you disqualified from the lender's "workout" assistance, and from federal or state assistance. If you do choose this route, be sure the rental income is sufficient to keep your loan current.

What to Do if Disaster Strikes

First and foremost, take action as soon as you get into trouble. Do not, by any means, ignore the situation. Open all mail from your lender immediately and don't wait for the lender to act first. Instead, call them before you are thirty days late with a payment and elicit their support in avoiding foreclosure. In all correspondence and communications, stress your desire to amicably resolve the situation and get back on track. Here are a few other actions you should take immediately:

- Contact the Federal Housing Administration (FHA) (*www.fha.gov*) and your state's government housing administration office to find out what laws apply and what rights you hold as the homeowner. Also review your loan documents to see what the terms specify regarding late or missed payments.
- Contact the U.S. Department of Housing and Urban Development (HUD) to inquire about free or very low-cost counseling. Housing counselors can help you understand the law and your options, organize your finances, and, if necessary, represent you in negotiations with your lender. Call them toll-free (800) 569-4287 or visit *www.hud.gov* to locate a center near you.

- Pay the mortgage first. After health care, food, and utilities, make house payments your first priority. Review your finances immediately, and drastically cut wherever you can to accumulate funds. Basically, ratchet down everything, including cable, cell phones, clothing, entertainment, and so on.
- Don't pay your credit card bills. Credit card debt is unsecured debt, i.e., the credit card company has loaned you money without requiring a secure asset to cover the debt. Mortgage is a secured debt, i.e., your house is the secured asset for your mortgage. Thus, your mortgage takes precedence over any "unsecured" debt. If you don't pay your credit card bill, you will incur late charges, but they cannot take your house if you fail to pay. If you don't pay your mortgage, eventually they will take your house.
- Sell expendable assets. If you have assets that you can sell, including a whole life insurance policy that has accumulated cash value, consider liquidating them as soon as you can and using the funds to reinstate your loan. See Chapter 9 for more information about whole life insurance policy options and whether you should cash out.
- Find an extra job. If you, or anyone else in the family, can secure an extra job, make it happen as soon as possible. Even if it's not enough to make the full payment, this kind of drastic action will demonstrate to your lender that you are willing to make sacrifices to keep your home.

Credit counselors can often negotiate reduced payments or long-term payment plans with your creditors. Beware of credit counseling agencies that offer counseling for a large upfront fee or donation. The majority of credit counseling agencies are reputable and provide their services free of charge, or for a small monthly administrative fee tied to a repayment plan. Several of these agencies include:

- National Credit Foundation for Credit Counseling (*www.nfcc.org*)
- Hope Now (*www.hopenow.com*)
- HUD Approved Counseling Agencies (*www.hud.gov*)

ONE-INCOME INQUIRY

Where can I find free or low-cost counseling?
While some government agencies limit their counseling services to homeowners with Federal Housing Administration (FHA) assisted mortgages, many others offer free help to anyone. Call the HUD local office or the housing authority in your state, city, or county for help. You can also contact the NeighborWorks Center for Foreclosure Solutions at (888) 995-HOPE or *http://nw.org*. The Center is an initiative of NeighborWorks America, a reputable resource for foreclosure assistance.

Negotiate with the Lender

As soon as you are in a position in which you cannot make a house payment, particularly if you know that this may be the first of several months when this will occur, it is extremely important that you call your lender. If you alert them to your circumstances, they may be willing to negotiate a payment plan. Keep in mind that lenders don't want to foreclose on properties. They have a vested interest in helping you succeed, but they cannot help if they don't know that there's a problem. Begin by gathering the following information:

- Your loan account number.
- Your home equity. Calculate this by estimating the current market value of your home, and then deducting the balance of your first and any second mortgage or home equity loan.
- Any documentation that explains your present circumstances, along with a brief explanation of your circumstances and whether you expect them to be short-term, long-term, or permanent.

- Recent income documents such as pay stubs as well as benefit statements from social security, disability, unemployment, retirement, or public assistance. If you are self-employed, have your tax returns or a year-to-date profit and loss statement available for reference.
- A list of household expenses.
- A list of debtors, secured loans, and credit cards.
- An idea about what you would like to see happen: You want to keep your home or you are willing to surrender the home, but want to salvage your equity and credit rating.
- A realistic assessment of what you can reasonably pay per month.

When you initiate a conversation with your loan company or assistance program, do the following:

- Keep extensive notes of all communications, including date and time of contact; the nature of the contact (phone, e-mail, fax), the name and title of the representative you spoke to; and the agreed-upon outcome.
- Immediately follow up with a letter verifying your conversation—via certified mail, return receipt requested. Keep copies of your letter and any enclosures.
- Meet all agreed-upon deadlines.

When you negotiate with a lender, they may offer several alternatives to foreclosure. Remember, it's very important that you seek additional counseling before deciding on a course of action.

Forbearance

Forbearance means that your lender agrees to forestall taking legal action, such as the filing of a Notice of Default, if you offer—and implement—a realistic repayment plan. In this case, your lender may allow you to reduce or suspend payments for a short period of time after which another option must be agreed upon to bring your loan current. A forbearance option is often combined with a reinstatement, which occurs when you know you will have enough money to bring the account current at a specific time in the future, based on known income, such as a hiring bonus, investment return, an insurance settlement, or a tax refund.

A Repayment Plan

If you can reassure and provide proof that you can maintain payments from a certain point forward, the lender may consider a long-term repayment plan for the missed payments, such as allowing you to tack on an extra $100 per month until they are repaid.

Call your lender and ask to speak with a *supervisor* in the loss mitigation department. Ask for a repayment plan. You will need to come up with some money to make a couple of payments under the repayment plan to demonstrate good faith in paying the mortgage. Once you have demonstrated that you are willing to try to bring the loan current, the lender will most likely work with you on a modification of terms. Generally there is only a small fee, roughly $200, to do this.

ONE-INCOME INQUIRY

Should I deal with foreclosure prevention companies?
No. Many for-profit companies will contact you promising to negotiate a solution with your lender. While these may be legitimate businesses, they will charge you a hefty fee (often equivalent to two or three months' mortgage payments) for information and services that your lender or an approved housing counselor will provide free if you contact them. You don't need to pay fees for foreclosure prevention help—use that money to pay the mortgage instead.

If the loan was an adjustable rate and your mortgage history was perfect prior to the rate increase, you may be eligible for a program called FHA Secure, which is designed for this type of situation. This is a regular refinance of the existing loan. It is not, however, a subprime loan or private money, so the terms are very reasonable.

Change the Terms of Your Loan

If your mortgage is an adjustable loan, the lender may be willing to freeze or lower your interest rate. A lender might also agree to modify your loan by extending the amortization period. Amortization is the number of equal monthly payments of principal and interest you make over a specified period of time. Interest on amortized loans is paid in arrears, and more interest is paid during the early period of the loan than at the end of the loan. Borrowers can shorten loan periods by paying more principal with each payment.

Add the Back Payments to Your Loan Balance

If you have sufficient equity and meet the company's lending guidelines, the lender might increase your loan balance to include the back payments and re-amortize the loan. This equates to refinancing, without the cost of normal refinancing.

Knowledge
is Power
◀ If you have a mortgage through the Federal Housing Administration (FHA) or Veterans Administration (VA), you may have other foreclosure alternatives. Contact the FHA (*www.fha.gov*) or VA (*http://homeloans.va.gov*) to discuss your options.

Offer to Take a Separate Loan for the Missed Payments

Certain government loans contain provisions that let borrowers who meet specific criteria apply for another loan to pay back the missed payments. Lenders refer to this as a partial claim. You might also qualify for a claim advance: If your mortgage is insured, you may be able to obtain an interest-free loan from your mortgage guarantor to bring your account current. The repayment of this loan may be delayed for several years.

Ask the Lender to Forgive the Missed Payments

If you can convince the lender that the inability to pay was a one- or two-time occurrence that will not happen again and that your circumstances will make it impossible for you to make up the lost payments, they may forgive the missed payments. Don't count on this, however, as circumstances rarely warrant this reprieve.

If you and the lender cannot agree on a specific type of loan modification or if your request for forbearance is denied, you should immediately contact legal counsel for assistance. When selecting an attorney, be sure to obtain the services of someone who has experience dealing with foreclosure cases.

Recent Changes That May Help

The Emergency Economic Stabilization Act (passed in February 2009) provides measures to help homeowners avoid foreclosure: One measure is a refinancing program aimed at homeowners with less than 20 percent equity in their home or whose mortgages are for more than their home is now worth. Another measure is designed to help "at-risk" homeowners lower their monthly payments to affordable levels to minimize the impact of foreclosure. Because these programs have only recently taken effect, many of the details were being worked out at press time. Begin by seeking the most up-to-date information at *www.treas.gov/initiatives/eesa* and *www.financialstability.gov*.

Last-Gasp Strategies

If you are beyond the point at which you could negotiate with the lender, and they have proceeded to file a Notice of Default, your options are limited. You will be given a certain time period to bring the payments current (including interest) and to pay the lender's costs of filing the foreclosure, thereby stopping it. They would then reinstate your loan. If you cannot make up the missed payments and the lender will not work with you, you may be able to stop foreclosure by one of the following means.

Secure the Right to Occupy the House

The lender may be willing to extend the period of time you can remain in the house. Since you essentially have the right to remain in the house anyway, lenders are often willing to allow you to remain until the house sells. This may make it easier for them to sell the house, and give you time to find another place to live. Since some owners trash the property before they vacate, your lender may be more amenable to this arrangement if you sign a contract to surrender the property in optimum condition.

Sell Your House

If the real estate market is in an upswing and your property has maximum marketing potential, you may want to negotiate with the lender to be given time to sell the house. Your lender will usually agree to give you a specific amount of time to find a purchaser and pay off the total amount owed, but they will require that you obtain the services of a real estate professional to aggressively market the property. To make this argument, ask your real estate agent to prepare a report on the house's market value and the average number of days listings are active, known as days on the market (DOM), before they have a pending sale. In really hot markets, houses can sell the day they go on the market and a favorable report will bolster your case. Also, keep in mind that your lender may consent to allow a qualified buyer to assume your mortgage, even if your original loan documents state that it is nonassumable.

Surrender the Deed to Settle the Debt

The lender may agree to accept the deed in lieu of foreclosure. Essentially, you negotiate with the lender to cancel the foreclosure and accept a properly prepared and notarized deed as payment of the outstanding loan. This may sound like the easiest way to stop foreclosure; however, most lenders will require that you attempt to sell the home for its fair market value for at least ninety days before they consider this option. Also, if you have other liens, such as judgments of other creditors, second mortgages, or Internal Revenue Service (IRS) or state tax liens, they aren't likely to agree to this solution. It's important to keep in mind that even if the lender does agree, your credit rating will be negatively affected. Still, you may want to explore the advantages, if any, with a real estate lawyer or HUD counselor.

Investigate a Short Sale

If you are on the brink of foreclosure, you may be offered an opportunity to negotiate a short sale. Basically, your lender may decide to "settle" for less than the amount owed. It's important to note that lenders don't typically accept a short sale until you are already several payments behind and on the brink of foreclosure. They generally restrict short sales to situations in which there is not enough equity to cover the costs of selling the house, and in which the seller does not have any other cash assets to bridge the gap.

| Knowledge is Power | If you're a seller trying to decide whether to let a home go through foreclosure versus attempting a short sale to limit damage to your credit or FICO score, weigh the advantages carefully. According to experts, there's no credit score advantage to a short sale versus a foreclosure. |

But is a short sale the smart thing to do? According to experts, a short sale has several deleterious effects:

- The effect of a short sale on a seller's credit rating is identical to that of a foreclosure. In other words, both will lower your credit score. A short sale will be recorded as "a pre-foreclosure in redemption status" or "settled for less than owed" and will cause a serious drop of 200 to 300 points in your FICO score, virtually identical to the dip a foreclosure causes.

- A short sale will make it difficult to impossible to obtain an institutional loan at an affordable interest rate for roughly three to five years—the same as for a foreclosure. This applies whether or not you boosted your FICO score significantly after the short sale. Also, Fannie Mae guidelines require a time period of two years that must elapse before borrowers can demonstrate that they have re-established an acceptable credit history after the short sale.

- Except for certain conditions pursuant to the Mortgage Forgiveness Debt Relief Act of 2007, the IRS may consider the amount of debt the lender forgives as income, making you subject to increased taxes. However, there are also several exceptions and exclusions that may allow part or all of the income resulting from the cancellation of debt to be considered nontaxable.

- The lender may have legal recourse to seek a deficiency judgment, which means they can sue you for the difference between the loan amount and the amount received from the short sale, i.e., if your loan amount is $246,000, and you only netted $200,000 from the short sale, you will still owe the mortgage company $246,000. Some states protect the seller on the original purchase loan, but equity loans, refinanced loans, and hard-money loans may be open game. Also, some states consider a "personal guarantee" that may be included in the original loan documents as an inviolable need to repay the full loan.

Often real estate brokers or salespersons do not fully understand the full consequences you will face with a short sale. Thus, it is always wise to consult with an accountant regarding possible taxation, and a real estate lawyer to ascertain the likelihood of deficiency judgment or other ramifications of a short sale.

If you decide that a short sale is your best course of action, you'll need to prepare and collect the following:

- Obtain the name of the person who handles short sales for the lender. To minimize frustration, make the necessary calls to reach the person who is capable of making the final decision. Otherwise, you will waste time pitching the idea to the wrong people.
- Send a letter to the lender authorizing them to negotiate directly with your real estate lawyer, the closing agent, and the title company. Make sure you provide the property address, the loan number, your name as it appears on the loan documents, the current date, and your real estate agent's and lawyer's name and contact information.
- Ask your closing agent or lawyer to prepare an estimated closing statement that shows the expected sale price, the costs involved, any unpaid loan balances, outstanding payments due, late fees incurred, and the real estate commissions that will be paid. Obviously, if the sale price exceeds the costs, you won't be eligible for a short sale.
- Write a letter outlining your current circumstances and need for a short sale. Don't exaggerate, but do be forthright and honest. Lenders may make a far more favorable decision based on the circumstances that have brought you to this dire situation.
- Enclose a simple balance sheet. The lender will request and is entitled to an honest accounting of your assets and your liabilities. Assets include other property owned (real estate or valuable assets, such as an art collection or a vintage automobile), savings accounts, money market accounts, stocks or bonds, and cash. Again, if your assets exceed your liabilities, you may not be

eligible for a short sale; or the lender may attempt to secure payment through liquidation of tangible assets.

- Enclose the last six months' bank statements and explain any large deposits, cash withdrawals, or flurry of checks.
- Have your realtor prepare a comparative market analysis (CMA). If real estate values have dropped drastically in your area, or if inventory and pending sales are particularly high, and your agent can document this by comparing your house to similar houses that sold under market value, this may sway the lender to accept a short sale.

Keep in mind that honesty is the best policy, and that failing to be honest may result in a lawsuit. If you secure a short sale, you will need to send a copy of the offer, along with a copy of your listing agreement, to the lender. Before you accept an offer, ask the lender whether they will include some typical expenses, such as a termite inspection or home protection plans, that are often paid by the seller. They may also request a lower commission from the realtors, so you need to make sure that you won't be tapped for the difference.

Finally, if you have established an amicable, or at least professional relationship with the lender, ask them very politely if they would be willing to forgo a report to the credit reporting agencies. Although most do report a short sale, they are not legally required to do so.

File Bankruptcy

Since the ramifications of personal bankruptcy are long lasting and far reaching, this is usually your last resort. A bankruptcy remains on your credit report for ten years, which will make it almost impossible to obtain credit, buy another home, buy life insurance, or even find a job. However, if you haven't been able to work out any other solution, you may want to investigate filing Chapter 13 bankruptcy. As long as you have a regular income, Chapter 13 may allow you to keep your house or car. Basically, the court approves a repayment plan that allows you to use your future income toward payment of your debts during a three- to five-year period. After you have made all the payments under the plan, certain debts are discharged. To learn more about Chapter 13, log on to the U.S. Trustee Program at *www.usdoj.gov/ust*.

Be Wary of Foreclosure Rescue Scams

Unfortunately, scam artists prey upon those who are in financial trouble and who are emotionally susceptible to scare tactics or desperate for a lifeline rescue. These predatory scams include:

- **The Foreclosure Prevention Specialist:** The "specialist" is a phony counselor who charges outrageous fees in exchange for making phone calls or completing paperwork you could easily do yourself. Nothing they do will help you save your home. They are selling false hope, and wasting the time you need to spend seeking qualified help.
- **A Lease/Buy Back Agreement:** They promise to pay your mortgage and allow you to lease or buy the property back at a later date. They expect you to hand over your deed when you sign on, and the terms of their "agreement" will be so stringent that buying back will be impossible. Typically the victims are evicted, and the scammer walks off with most or all of their equity.
- **The Bait-and-Switch Tactic:** These scammers offer an agreement to bring your mortgage current for a reasonable price, but hidden language gives them ownership. Basically, you're handing over your deed, and you may not find out until an eviction notice arrives.

You can use the Internet to research options—which is a good idea, as long as you do not indiscriminately reveal your personal information. Be wary when you see flashing banners or lists of websites that offer help. It is extremely important that you do not reveal your personal information to anyone until you have verified that they are a legitimate business. If you suspect that the company badgering you for a quick fix is a scam, contact your state's department for real estate, your local district attorney's office for consumer fraud, and/or the FBI. Committing mortgage fraud is illegal.

You can also log on to the Federal Trade Commission (FTC) website: *http://ftc.gov/credit*. The FTC is your ally for discovering fraudulent, deceptive, and unfair business practices. You can also access free information on the U.S. government's portal to financial education: *http://mymoney.gov*. A more complete list of agencies can be found in Appendix C.

Tax Consequences of Debt Cancellation

In the past, if you borrowed money from a commercial lender and the lender later canceled or forgave the debt, in many cases, you were required to report the canceled amount as income for tax purposes. Due to the surge of foreclosures, the Mortgage Forgiveness Debt Relief Act of 2007 generally allows taxpayers to exclude income from the discharge of debt on their principal residence. This includes debt reduced through mortgage restructuring, as well as mortgage debt forgiven in connection with a foreclosure. This does *not* include debt forgiven on a second home, credit card, or car loans.

If you are having difficulty resolving a tax problem (such as one involving an IRS bill, letter, or notice) through normal IRS channels, the Taxpayer Advocate Service (TAS) may be able to help. For more information, call the TAS case intake line toll-free at (877) 777-4778, TTY/TDD (800) 829-4059. In some cases, you may qualify for free or low-cost assistance from a Low Income Taxpayer Clinic (LITC). These are independent organizations that represent low-income taxpayers in tax disputes with the IRS. Ask TAS for a referral.

Losses from the sale or foreclosure of personal property are not deductible.

What if Foreclosure Results in a Gain?

A reportable gain from foreclosure (foreclosures are treated like sales for tax purposes) may be taxable. Generally, the same tax rules apply as when you sell your home: If you have owned and used the home as your principal residence for periods totaling at least two years during the five-year period ending on the date of the foreclosure, you may exclude up to $250,000 (up to $500,000 for married couples filing a joint return) from income. If you do not qualify for this exclusion, or your gain exceeds $250,000 ($500,000 for married couples filing a joint return), report the taxable amount on Schedule D, Capital Gains and Losses.

Funding College

Chapter Eight

Saving Up for College • Options That Will Reduce Costs •
Applying for Financial Aid • Grants • Student Loans • Tax
Savings

IF YOU HAVE children, you will undoubtedly grapple with the cost of education. While the topic itself could—and does—fill many books, we will cover the basics and then refer you to books or websites that provide detailed information. You'll find these resources listed in Appendix C.

In today's world, your children need to go to college to compete successfully in an increasingly sophisticated global market. College may seem prohibitively expensive, but living on one income does not have to rule out college for your children—or for yourself. Obviously, if you have sufficient income to cover all of your expenses and enough left over to invest funds in a college account, kudos to you! However, if you cannot see any way to accumulate funds to pay for college, you'll want to broaden your knowledge of the options available.

Saving Up for College

When it comes to saving for your children's education, starting early is essential to building sufficient funds. There are tax-advantaged savings plans available to assist. Their basic allowances and qualifications are as follows:

- You can contribute $2,000 each year to a Coverdell Education Savings Account. Funds in the account grow tax-free, and can be spent on almost any education-related expense for your child as soon as she starts first grade.
- You can deposit significantly larger annual amounts, $235,000 plus, in 529 savings accounts earmarked for college expenses. Earnings grow tax-deferred and distributions are tax-free when used for qualified post-secondary education costs. However, to retain tax-free status on the account's gains, you must spend withdrawn funds on tuition, room and board, fees, books, supplies, and equipment used for college and graduate school—and not for elementary, junior, or high school education expenses.

- You can also take advantage of a Qualified Tuition Program (also a 529 plan). These 529 plans allow you to prepay your child's tuition directly to an approved state or educational institution—at today's prices. These Qualified Tuition 529 Plan contributions cannot be more than the amount necessary to provide for tuition fees, books, supplies, and equipment. One obvious drawback is that you have to know well in advance that your child will attend the college you select to maximize savings.

Educational savings bonds are a safe, tax-advantaged option, but typically don't accrue enough interest to bolster savings. Custodial accounts are an option, but they don't offer tax advantages, and can be problematic if your children obtain ownership at age eighteen or twenty-one and squander the funds. Using your Roth IRA to fund your child's education is possible, and may be reasonable if you are at least age 59½ when your child attends college, but isn't generally recommended because withdrawals from the account are counted by financial aid formulas as parental income and could limit access to additional financial aid. Also, using your Roth IRA may create a situation in which you have to choose between your retirement savings and your child's education.

Even if you are strapped for money, investing a small sum each month can add up. It might not pay for college, but accumulated savings can significantly reduce the costs, and thereby the amount of money you or your child will need to borrow. If there is any way you can open a savings account for each child and make small, regular deposits, by all means do it! As they get older, you can show your children how the money has accumulated and encourage them to add money earned through allowances or part-time work. You can also ask relatives to make contributions in lieu of birthday or Christmas presents.

Also, as you accumulate funds, if you have not used one of the ESA or 529 education savings' plans noted above, you may want to invest the saved funds in savings bonds, or deposit them in a higher-interest-rate money market account, or purchase a CD, or invest in low-risk investments, such as government bonds. Dependent upon the length of time before the funds will be tapped, you may want to investigate high-risk investments, such as stocks. If you are in this enviable position, consult with a financial adviser to explore your best options.

Since the majority of one-income households won't have the luxury of contributing to college investment plans, let's focus on how the average one-income household can still fund college.

Options That Will Reduce Costs

There are steps you can take to reduce the cost of your child's college education. Among them, of course, are having your child live at home for the first two years, achieve academic excellence to garner scholarships, take college classes while still in high school, and work while in college. It would be wise to maximize opportunities to keep the cost down for you, or to minimize the loan that your child will need to fund his or her education.

Community College and Junior College

Many communities have a local community college, or a junior college, that offers two-year associate's degree programs. Typically, these include an associate of arts, an associate of science, or an associate of applied science. Often, your child can live at home and take classes for a much lower cost-per-credit fee than at a four-year college. As long as the college is accredited by an agency recognized by the U.S. Secretary of Education and is eligible for federal student aid programs, the earned credits usually can be transferred to a four-year college.

Other benefits of a community or junior college are that a high school diploma isn't necessary to attend, and they usually offer a lower price to local students than to out-of-town students. Many of these schools have viable programs and an outstanding reputation. Instead of feeling deprived that they have to attend the local school, students can take pride in receiving what is often a stellar education at an affordable price, which makes perfect sense for everyone.

It's important to validate the college's accreditation and consult with the school counselor to make sure that the student will be taking classes that provide the requirements needed to transfer to the four-year college of her choice.

Co-op Education

Many colleges will allow students to alternate a semester of school with a full-time job that relates to their course of study. This will increase the time spent attending college, but most likely only by one year or slightly more than one year. That way, the student can earn money and gain valuable work experience that will help him land a better job when he earns his degree. Also, some schools permit work experience to count as class credits.

Some schools will allow students to accelerate their education, earning a college degree in three instead of four years. To participate, the student has to illustrate an ability to handle the extra coursework and be able to attend school year-round.

Another form of acceleration is to earn college credits while still in high school, which can help by reducing the cost per credit or by shortening the length of time the student is in college. Students can do this by taking certain academic tests or taking classes known as advanced placement (AP) or College Level Exam Program (CLEP) courses. However, make sure that the college your child will attend recognizes the AP or CLEP courses or exams. If it doesn't, he would have to take the courses again, which wouldn't save you any money.

Working While in College

While the idea is for your child to be able to attend college without working, there are real benefits to having him work, at least part-time.

The most obvious is that it will save you—or him—money. The less you or your child has to borrow for college, the better. Student loans are not absolvable and must be repaid, and interest rates are likely to increase over the ten years or so it requires to repay the debt.

Scholarships

While your child is still a junior in high school, ask his high school counselor for a list of scholarships and other aid for which he can apply. Once your child selects a college, ask the college's financial aid administrator about financial aid available from the school itself, as well as other sources. Also, use online resources, such as the free scholarship search available on *http://studentaid.ed.gov.*

Other sources for scholarships include the following:

- National, state, and regional foundations and civic groups
- Local, community, religious, and ethnicity-based organizations
- Academic associations (which reward academic excellence)
- Professional associations related to your child's field of interest, such as the American Medical Association or American Bar Association
- Your employer and/or your child's employer
- Your union and/or your child's union
- Programs such as Upward Bound, Talent Search, or GEAR UP

There are a vast number of scholarships available, and some go untapped. Be sure to explore all your options, as winning a scholarship can vastly reduce the amount you will need to borrow.

Tuition Payment Plans

Presuming you have sufficient funds to pay for your child's education, you can ask the college if it accepts tuition payment plans. If so, the financial aid office will provide a list of companies that provide the service. Since it's not a loan, you don't have to file loan applications or even have a decent credit rating. What you do have to do is make regular payments over a ten-month or two-semester period to cover tuition. These plans may have a nominal annual cost, around $100, and allow you to budget for the payments rather than having to come up with one or two lump sums twice a year.

Applying for Financial Aid

Take heart in knowing that approximately 60 percent of undergraduates enrolled full-time in college receive financial aid. When it's time to finance your child's education, your primary source of information should be the U.S. Department of Education (*http://studentaid.ed.gov*). Federal student aid programs are the largest source of such aid in America, providing more than $80 billion a year in grants, loans, and work-study assistance.

There are many options available for financial aid, including federal and state loans and grants. The process can feel very intimidating, but it's well worth the effort to research options and to apply for virtually everything for which your child qualifies. Since these options are constantly changing, it's best to spend time researching online or at your local library. You'll find many books on the subject, but to get you started (and put your mind at rest) we'll cover some of the basics here.

Determine the School's Annual Cost of Attendance (COA)

Every school calculates its COA each year. This typically includes the tuition, room and board, books and supplies, travel to and from school, and some basic personal expenses. Often the COA is not as high as you imagine. Of course this amount changes annually, and there are always extra costs, such as lab or athletic fees, the cost of a computer, insurance, off-campus housing (if needed), transportation, clothing, and so on. It is always helpful to ascertain how much the COA has gone up annually for at least the five years preceding your child's entry into the system.

You can estimate the costs for your child's education by using a calculator on *www.finaid.org/calculators/costprojector.phtml*.

ONE-INCOME INQUIRY

Where do I find a school's COA?
You can frequently find a school's current COA on its website. If not, place a call to the financial aid office to inquire. Most schools will happily provide all available information to help you make the right financial decisions for your family.

File a Free Application for Federal Student Aid

The common denominator with all federal aid programs is the Free Application for Federal Student Aid (FAFSA), a document your student must file each year detailing her income, financial resources (as well as yours while she is your dependent), and college costs. The FAFSA filing establishes your child's Expected Family Contribution (EFC), a figure commonly used in federal financial aid calculations. The federal and state governments, and the colleges, as subsidized grantors or lenders, will require that your student submit a FAFSA to the federal government to process loan applications. Applications are available at your child's high school guidance offices in November or December or can be acquired online at *www.fafsa.ed.gov.*

Applications should be submitted as soon as possible after January 1, *not* prior to January 1. The deadline for applications is June 30, but obviously, applying late may jeopardize your child's chances of acquiring a loan. You will need to have extensive financial information handy, so be sure to review the information requested before going online to fill out the application.

Approximately four to six weeks after your student's FAFSA is filed, you should receive a Student Aid Report (SAR), which will indicate your EFC and detail your child's eligibility for federal aid programs. This information will be relayed to the six colleges your child selected. It is very important to carefully review the SAR for errors and ask for corrections immediately. Failing to do so can delay loan processing.

Knowledge is Power

It's important to make sure your child's preferred college is accredited. If the secretary of state where the school is located does not have the college on its list of accredited schools, your student will not be eligible for federal or state financial aid. To verify a school's status, call (800) 4FEDAID.

Determine Your Expected Family Contribution

This is the minimum amount your family will be expected to contribute toward the cost of college. You SAR will provide this number based on a standardized formula established by Congress. It is based on your income, assets, expenses, and number of children. Note that retirement funds and home equity are usually exempt from asset computations. Lenders and schools use these standards to determine how much they believe your family is capable of paying, and then employ this rating to determine qualifications for financial aid. Most schools and colleges use your EFC to determine eligibility for grants, scholarships, low-cost financial aid, work-study programs, or other cost-saving programs. Note: Financial aid usually needs to be reapplied for annually, and any changes in your financial status will affect eligibility requirements.

ONE-INCOME INQUIRY

What if my child works while attending school?
If your child works while attending college, half of his after-tax income above $2,200 will be added to your EFC. Weigh this when considering whether it really pays for him to work.

Most colleges expect students funding their own way through school to pay up to 35 percent of their personal assets and 50 percent of their income toward the cost of college. Parents funding college for their children or dependents are usually expected to spend 5.6 percent of their assets and a portion of available income based on their profile: age (how close you are to retirement), size of family (larger families obviously have greater expenses), and number of children in college. Allowances for health care costs and taxes are also taken into consideration.

Determine Your Unmet Needs

The term "unmet needs" applies to the financial shortfall that you will need to cover. Your options at this stage include:

- **Additional Scholarships.** Community or organizational scholarships that your student may win based on academic excellence, economic need, or various affiliations.
- **Additional Student Loans.** This would include federal and state loans available to the student, irrespective of financial need, or traditional bank loans to the student or the parent.
- **Tuition Assistance.** Some employers offer loans to dependents or to employees seeking additional education. Be sure to explore this option if it is available.
- **Asset-Based Loans.** You may be able to acquire a loan through your whole life insurance, home equity, or retirement fund. Since these loans tap your most precious assets—your whole life premium, your retirement account, and your house—these are less than ideal. Basically, unless you have the ability to repay these loans rather quickly, try every other avenue first.

Grants

Ideally, your children will be eligible for federal, state, or institutional grants that will cover a large portion of their college expenses. A grant means free money—money that doesn't have to be paid back. Your two prime federal opportunities are a Pell Grant or a Supplemental Education Opportunity Grant.

| Knowledge is Power | Supplemental Education Opportunity Grants and Perkins Loans are offered by your student's college on a *first come, first served basis*. To make sure you don't miss out on these programs, find out the earliest possible date to submit your student's FAFSA documents to the college(s) of her choice, sign up for PIN numbers for yourself and her through *www.fafsa.ed.gov*, and submit all requested information via the same website as close as possible to that date. |

Pell Grants

The federal government offers annual Pell Grants to students with "exceptional financial need," and they are the most popular form of student aid—traditionally claimed by approximately 5 million students each year. Your family's EFC determines the depth of need. If you qualify for a Pell Grant, you will warrant a grant that may range from $400 to $4,731 (in 2008–2009) based on your family's financial need, the COA of your child's college, the length of your child's education, and whether your student will be attending full-time or part-time. The maximum can change each award year and depends on program funding. This is a federal grant and thus not dependent on the college's resources. You must reapply annually.

Federal Supplemental Education Opportunity Grant (FSEOG)

The federal government also gives participating colleges a fixed amount of money each year to fund FSEOG grants. The colleges distribute these funds as part of their financial aid packages. Typically,

FSEOG grants are awarded to those students with the greatest financial need—on a *first come, first served* basis. Qualified students receive $100 to $4,000 a year. You must apply for a Pell Grant, or at least qualify for a Pell Grant, before applying for an FSEOG. The U.S. Department of Education recommends that the first eligible group for FSEOG be made up of Pell Grant–eligible students with the lowest EFC; after all Pell-eligible students are taken care of by the program, the next class of students to receive funds is non-Pell students who have the lowest EFCs.

If you hope to secure this grant for your child, make sure that any college your student is considering participates in this program before making your final selection.

Knowledge is Power

Steer clear of websites that offer scholarship or funding resource searches. These typically require fees that simply aren't necessary; despite their claims, they cannot guarantee that you'll be awarded anything, and the website may be the front for a scam. Never, ever reveal your financial information online before thoroughly checking out the legitimacy of the company or organization! Save yourself money by conducting your own research and by asking your child's high school guidance counselor and the college's financial aid office for references.

Federal Work-Study Programs

While not technically a grant, federal work-study programs are a way to subsidize college expenses. Basically, the program is available as part of a financial aid package, which means the college decides which students are eligible, based on financial need. Typically, the jobs pay minimum wage, or slightly higher, and require ten to twenty hours of employment per week, usually on campus. The earnings are allocated toward your child's expenses, allowing you to minimize loans that will need to be repaid.

Also, you may be able to have a portion of college expenses covered if your student pursues a particular field of study, volunteers to teach in inner-city schools, or joins the Peace Corps. The federal—and some state—governments may absolve some or all of your federal or state loans if your child pursues a career in teaching or health care, or in other fields where shortages exist. National and community service programs, paid for by the federal government but run by schools and outside organizations, typically require your student to commit to work a minimum of forty-two weeks a year for two to four years. They do provide an income, plus living expenses, but there are a lot of stipulations, so it's best to review such programs in light of your and your child's situation. You can find more about these programs and their stipulations at:

http://studentaid.ed.gov/PORTALSWebApp/students/english/cancelstaff.jsp

www.civicmind.com/service.htm

In addition, the federal government offers internships or fellowships at the high school and college levels. In high school, inquire at the counselor's office; in college, inquire at the financial aid office.

Student Loans

Although it may be scary, your child can borrow money using federally subsidized loans. These loans are awarded based on financial need (determined by your EFC and FAFSA). Although student loans are frequently necessary, there are two *golden rules* of borrowing that you should urge your child to follow.

1. Never borrow more than you need. Padding the amount so she can live in a better apartment or not work for four years means that your student will be overwhelmed with debt just when she finally starts to make money.

2. Borrow only what she can realistically repay. Again, borrowing more than she will realistically be able to repay can mean years of painful niggling—with no reprieve.

Federal Loans

There are several subsidized federal loan programs that your child may be able to resource. Subsidized federal loans are awarded based on financial need, and usually offer lower interest rates. The government pays the interest while your child is attending college and during the grace period (six to nine months after graduation). The three subsidized federal loans are as follows:

- **Federal Perkins Loan.** This loan is usually available at the lowest rates possible, and the beginning of the payback is deferred until nine months after graduation. Your child can borrow $4,000 per year up to $20,000 for undergraduate education and has ten years to repay the loan. The student repays the school directly. Perkins Loans are offered on a *first come, first served basis*, so it's imperative that students apply as soon as possible.
- **Stafford Loans, also known as Federal Family Education Loan (FFEL).** These loans are awarded from commercial lenders, but the federal government pays the interest until six months after your child graduates. Interest rates are usually higher than the Federal Perkins Loan, but students have ten to twenty-five years for repayment.
- **Federal Direct Loan.** This is equal to the Stafford Loan (FFEL), except the government pays the money directly to the college, and the borrower later repays the government instead of a commercial lender. Like the FFEL, students have ten to twenty-five years for repayment.

Colleges don't generally offer all three options, but most provide at least one. Be aware that the loans require a guarantee and must be repaid. Your child will probably be asked to sign a Master Promissory Note, which states the terms and conditions. Be sure to read this document thoroughly. Most student loans are not absolved by bankruptcy, so your child must be prepared to repay the loan in its entirety—even if she drops out of school or doesn't earn a degree.

State Loans

Like the federal government, all state governments offer need-based loans, and some offer merit-based scholarships. Many states also have work-study programs and loan alleviation programs, dependent upon career choice. If your child wants to attend college in another state, you may be able to find "reciprocal" fees, which allow students to pay the same reduced tuition as their resident students. Some states will also allow you to make payments toward your child's education at present-day prices; however, these funds are usually nonrefundable, which means if your child does not attend that particular state college, you may forfeit the payments. For information on the various options available in your state, visit the state government's website and look for its educational agency page.

Unsubsidized Loans

If neither you nor your child qualifies for the federally subsidized loans, you can apply for unsubsidized Parent Loans for Undergraduate Students (PLUS) loans. These loans do not require a financial need; the parents only need an acceptable credit rating to be approved. Two federal loan programs are available to parents.

- **Direct PLUS.** The federal government (the U. S. Department of Education) pays the college directly in installments; and (after their child graduates) the parents repay the college.

- **FFEL PLUS.** The parents secure a loan from an approved lender; the lender pays your child's college expenses. After they graduate, you (or your child) repay the lender.

Since the government does not subsidize these loans, you will likely pay a higher interest rate (usually they cannot exceed 8.5 percent) and may pay additional fees that may equate to 4–5 percent of the loan amount. The repayment period also activates sooner than subsidized loans, usually within sixty days after graduation, and interest usually begins to accrue the day you acquire the loan. If you ask for a deferment, the lender usually adds the interest accumulated while your student is in college to the amount owed, which means you will pay interest on your interest. You may be able to counteract this with tax deductions, but it's wise to be aware of the difference between a subsidized and an unsubsidized loan. FFEL PLUS loans allow repayment based on the amount of income you earn. Families can select an "income-sensitive" repayment plan with higher payments when family income is higher and lower payments when income is less.

ONE-INCOME INQUIRY

Can I deduct student loan interest?

Tax benefits are available for certain higher education expenses, including a deduction for student loan interest for certain borrowers. The maximum deduction is $2,500 a year. For more information, review Internal Revenue Service (IRS) Publication 970, Tax Benefits for Education, available on *www.irs.gov* or by calling (800) 829-1040. You can also consult with a financial or tax adviser.

If you don't qualify for an unsubsidized PLUS loan, your child may be able to obtain an unsubsidized FFEL or Stafford loan. Unlike the PLUS loan applications, these require a FAFSA. Again, interest is accrued from the date the loan is acquired and can be deferred, as with the PLUS loans, but will be added to the amount owed.

Commercial Loans

If none of the previous options is available, you can apply for commercial loans. Many banks, credit unions, and student loan companies are eager to loan money to you or your student. Although these are typically competitive with federally subsidized or unsubsidized loans, you may pay additional fees of up to 5 percent for a "guarantee" (this may be refundable if you repay the loan) and up to 7 percent in origination fees. Since there have been recent reports of unsavory lenders, it is important that you make sure the lending institution or loan company is reputable. Ask the college's financial aid office for a list of credible lenders, and thoroughly review all loan documents, looking for hidden charges.

ONE-INCOME INQUIRY

How Much Debt Is Acceptable?

Lenders will assess your creditworthiness based on three numbers: your cost for housing, your outstanding loans, and your total debt. Basically, they want your housing costs (mortgages plus any equity loans, or rent) to be no more than 28 percent of your take-home pay. They also prefer that no more than 9 percent of your take-home pay is allocated for other recurring loans (car loans, credit card payments, other student loans, and so on). That means your total debt should not exceed 37 percent of your take-home pay.

Two of the most well-known lending agencies are the Student Loan Marketing Association, more commonly known as Sallie Mae (*http://salliemae.com*), and the nonprofit agency known as Nellie Mae (*www.nelliemae.org*).

Repaying Student Loans

Student loans are readily available and strenuously protected. Even if you declare bankruptcy, your student loans must be repaid. Your loan is considered in default if you fail to make payments according to the terms of your promissory note. You do have options to forestall default, including the following:

1. **Deferment.** You may able to defer or suspend payments if you are facing a hardship. Ask your loan bearer if they would be willing to defer payments (and interest) until you can resolve the situation. In some cases, deferments may be available for up to three years. This does not apply to unsubsidized PLUS or Stafford loans.

2. **Forbearance.** If you don't qualify for a time-sensitive deferment, your loan bearer may consent to forbearance, which allows you to freeze payments for a period of time. The interest accrual still occurs, and you usually have a choice whether to pay the interest as it accrues, or to have it tacked onto the amount of the loan.

3. **Graduated payments.** Your loan bearer may agree to let you pay less initially and slowly raise the amount you pay as your earning potential increases.

4. **Income-sensitive payments.** Your loan bearer may agree to increase or decrease your payments according to increases or decreases in your income.

5. **Extended payments.** Your lender might agree to extend payments over fifteen, twenty-five, or even thirty years rather than the standard ten years. This usually applies to loans above $20,000, but it never hurts to ask.

6. **Consolidation.** Many students eventually refinance by consolidating their various loans into one, ideally one with a lower interest rate and/or a longer period of time in which to repay the loan. Consolidation loans vary, but there are limits to how much interest they can charge. Make sure you shop around for the best interest rate. This is also a good time to negotiate better repayment options, such as those discussed in this list.

If you default on your student loan(s), the lender or agency has the right to take all necessary action to recover payment. They will likely notify the national credit bureaus, which will negatively affect your credit rating and make it very difficult for you to obtain credit for any purpose. Also, they may be able to require your employer to make automatic deductions from your earnings, or to have the IRS withhold any refunds. Defaulting would also make it impossible to acquire new educational loans.

Knowledge is Power ◀ | If you pay interest on a non-federal loan that you are liable for, you are able to deduct the interest on your taxes. Scholarship money used for tuition and course-related expenses are tax-free; however, funds received and used to pay room and board are taxable.

Tax Savings

Since our society values higher education, the government offers financial support in the form of tax credits. While tax deductions reduce your taxable income, tax credits are subtracted from the amount of taxes you pay, and thus are more valuable. There are multiple tax credits for which you may qualify.

Hope Credit

This is not really a scholarship, but it is a way for the government to provide a tax credit that helps parents afford college for their children. It is a nonrefundable credit that can be used to off-set taxes you owe for qualified expenses up to $1,000, plus half of expenses over $1,000, with a maximum credit amount of $1,500. Qualified expenses include tuition and required fees for you or your dependent to attend the first two years of a qualified postsecondary school (one that is eligible to disburse federal financial aid) and required books or supplies purchased directly from the college or school.

Since this is a tax credit, rather than a tax deduction, parents can directly subtract this amount from the taxes they owe. Here are the basic eligibility guidelines:

- The student must be attending a qualified college at least part-time.
- The student must be a freshman or sophomore.
- The student must have a clear record; in other words, no felony counts or drug offenses during that tax year.

The taxpayers have to request a form from their child's college that describes their eligible expenses to submit to the IRS. You must owe taxes, claim the student as a dependent, and owe less in taxes than the maximum credit available. If the parents are withdrawing money from an education IRA to cover college expenses, they may not be eligible for a Hope credit. Make sure to discuss this option with your tax preparer.

Lifetime Learning Credit

This is another tax credit (as opposed to a tax deduction) that provides support for those funding higher education for their child or dependent or themselves. Education expenses that qualify for the Hope credit also qualify for the lifetime learning credit; however, the lifetime learning credit is not restricted to the first two years of the student's higher education.

You cannot claim the Hope credit and the lifetime learning credit in the same year. But if you have more than one student in the family (including yourself), you could use the Hope credit for one and the lifetime learning credit for the other. If you or your child are in the first two years of college, the relevant qualifying expenses are under $7,500 for the calendar year. If you have to decide between the lifetime learning credit and the Hope credit, keep in mind that the Hope credit offers greater financial rewards. If qualified expenses paid are over $7,500, the higher-limit lifetime learning credit ($2,000 maximum) is the better choice.

The lifetime learning credit has fewer qualifying restrictions than does the Hope credit. For instance, the student is not required to pursue a degree or certificate, and the student remains qualified regardless of whether she has a felony drug offense on her record.

Loan Interest Deductions

The federal government also allows you to deduct up to $2,500 in education loan interest. This deduction will lower in relation to your income. If your adjusted gross income (AGI) is between $55,000 and $70,000 (for a single, in 2008) or between $115,000 and $145,000 (married, filing jointly in 2008), the deduction will be phased out. If your income is too high, you may be able to borrow in the student's name, but this precludes your ability to claim her as a dependent.

Navigating Health, Life, and Disability Insurance

Chapter Nine

Health and Dental Insurance Basics • Life Insurance Basics
• Disability Insurance Basics

WHEN YOU GO from two incomes to one, the desire to pare down costs may lead you to consider eliminating or reducing your insurance coverage. While you may be able to trim costs, or even eliminate certain types of insurance, there are essential needs, and the three primary ones are health and dental insurance, life insurance, and disability insurance.

In an ideal world, you would have maximum insurance coverage. In reality, a person or family relying on one income will likely have to make crucial decisions between what they cannot afford to be without and what they can realistically afford. However, even if you take every precaution to protect yourself and your family, you simply cannot presume that you're invincible to the cruel tides of fate.

Health and Dental Insurance Basics

No matter your financial situation, maintaining health and dental insurance is an absolute must. Ideally, the wage earner will have employer-provided insurance that covers the entire family. If not, you'll need to find an affordable plan that will cover you and your children. In general, your health insurance options are:

- **Health Maintenance Organizations (HMOs).** HMOs typically offer an extensive network of participating physicians from which you choose a primary care physician to coordinate your care and refer you to specialists, as needed. Most require a copay (usually $10–$15) for doctor visits and prescriptions. HMOs can be sufficient for families that are generally healthy. They are cheaper than PPO plans and often provide more options.
- **Preferred Provider Organizations (PPOs).** PPOs charge on a fee-for-service basis. They give you greater rein in doctor selection and choosing whether or not you see a specialist or have certain medical tests. The insurer pays participating, or "in-network," doctors, hospitals, and health care providers a negotiated,

discounted fee for services. If you choose to see an "out-of-net-work" doctor, you will pay the difference between what your PPO would cover and that doctor's fees. You will have a larger selection of doctors and hospitals, but you pay a higher premium, and typically higher copays if you see a doctor outside the plan or opt for branded prescriptions.

- **High-Deductible Health Plans (HDHP).** Also known as catastrophic coverage, these plans provide limited health insurance benefits at a considerably lower cost. Premiums are much cheaper than standard HMO or PPO plans, but you will have a high annual deductible—$2,000, $5,000, or $10,000. You will pay all medical expenses until the annual deductible is met. When buying such a plan, it is extremely important that you carefully review the policy description and what it does and does not cover. If you are really strapped for money and this is all you can afford, it will protect you from bankruptcy should a tragedy occur or anyone becomes gravely ill.

- **Government Assistance Plans.** If you cannot afford health insurance, your children may qualify for the State Children's Health Insurance Program (SCHIP) or federal Medicaid assistance. Amazingly, according to the government, six out of ten families who are eligible never apply. In most states, if you earn less than $36,000, your children are eligible for low cost—and sometimes free—medical coverage. Under Medicaid, a family earning less than $17,600 gross income per year that has one child under the age of six qualifies for free health coverage for the child. Check *www.cms.hhs.gov/home/schip.asp* and *www.insure kidsnow.gov* or call (877) KIDS-NOW to see if you qualify.

Also, some states now provide free or discounted health insurance for low-income residents. In Massachusetts, for example, you have regular insurance, but the state pays for your coverage. Dependent upon your income, you may pay a portion of the monthly costs or copays for doctor visits and prescriptions. If you live in Massachusetts, you can access information on *www.mahealthconnector.org*.

What Are Flexible Spending Plans, and Why Would I Want One?

Flexible spending plans are optional plans that employers may be able to offer employees. Basically, you predetermine a set amount for your employer to withhold from your pre-tax wages, which you can then spend to cover medical and dental costs that your insurance doesn't cover. This can save you 15 to 35 percent a year on copays, deductibles, braces, caps, laser eye surgery, over-the-counter medications, and other health care expenses.

Knowledge is Power	Much like credit reporting agencies, there is a Medical Information Bureau, which collects personal medical data and then sells it to life, health, and disability insurance companies. The information the bureau gathers could fluctuate wildly, and may not even belong to you. Log on to *www.mib.com* or write to MIB, PO Box 105, Essex Station, Boston, MA 02112 to request a copy of your report. If you find errors, ask the bureau to make corrections.

The only drawback is that you have to predetermine an amount for the entire year. Also, in many cases, funds not spent within 14½ months are forfeited to the government, but you'll learn how to deal with this. It is far better to underestimate and adjust upward than to not participate at all. A flexible spending plan can offer significant savings, particularly if you know in advance that you, or members of your family, will need braces or glasses during the next year. Even if the deadline to use the funds is approaching and you still have $400 in the account, you are permitted to use the funds to buy over-the-counter drugs, such as aspirin, or prescription sunglasses.

One essential tip: Save all your receipts so you can document your spending.

What Is COBRA and When Do I Need It?

The Consolidated Omnibus Budget Reconciliation Act (COBRA) requires employers to offer health coverage to employees who are fired or who leave for any reason, even if it's to transition into part-time work. Employers that have more than twenty employees must offer you (and your family, if they have been covered under your plan) COBRA health coverage at their cost, plus 2 percent, for a period of eighteen months. Legally separated, divorced, or widowed spouses are eligible for thirty-six months of COBRA coverage.

What Is HIPAA?

The Health Insurance Portability and Accountability Act (HIPAA) was created to protect your access to health insurance. Under HIPAA, anyone leaving a group insurance plan is guaranteed coverage as long as they were covered for at least twelve months and switch health care providers within sixty-three days. One of the smartest things you can do is take advantage of COBRA and HIPAA to ensure that your family will not be turned down, or made to wait for coverage.

What Are Health Savings Accounts?

If you are self-employed, you can open a health savings account (HSA), which combines high deductible, catastrophic health insurance with a tax-favored savings plan. It works like this: You make a tax-deductible contribution each year to the HSA to cover medical bills. If you don't use the funds, they will accumulate and the maximum amount you can contribute changes annually per legislation (the amount typically increases to reflect inflation and/or increased costs), with no cap on how much you can have in the HSA. This option is best for healthy families who have enough money to cover basic medical expenses. If this is your best option, talk to your financial adviser and an insurance broker about how to make this plan a smart move for you.

ONE-INCOME INQUIRY

Do I have to be totally truthful on insurance applications?
Yes! Even if it's tempting, never lie on insurance applications. Most policies have clauses that will nullify the contract if you have failed to provide accurate information. If you have a crisis and they discover that you've lied, you could lose the policy, any anticipated coverage, and all the premiums you paid.

Saving Money on Health Insurance

If you, and your children, are in good health, you can opt for coverage with a large deductible. This means that you will pay the deductible before coverage begins, which is always a gamble, but in many cases it may be worth the risk. If it's the only way you can afford decent coverage, for example, or if your family is relatively young and very healthy, you may be able to live quite comfortably with a $1,000 or $2,000 deductible.

If your coverage includes "in-network" and "out-of-network" providers, it's cheaper to stick to the in-network providers. The same goes for "generic" versus "branded" prescriptions. Most of the time, the differences in quality are nominal.

You can find the best rates by comparison shopping on the Internet (start on your state's health insurance page). Many health insurance sites offer side-by-side comparisons that will give you an idea of what to expect. When you've done your homework and are ready to purchase, find a reputable broker.

Life Insurance Basics

Life insurance provides important protection for your loved ones. If you have dependents, particularly young children, it's crucial that you have minimal life insurance protection in place. Basic life insurance serves the following purposes:

- Replaces your income for dependents. If the person who provides the income dies, adequate life insurance will replace his or her income, including the equivalent of government- or employer-sponsored benefits. This coverage protects anyone dependent upon the wage earner.
- Pays funeral expenses.
- Pays probate and other estate administration costs.
- Pays debts and medical expenses not covered by health insurance.
- Pays federal and state "death" taxes.
- Provides an inheritance for your dependents.

There are two major types of life insurance—term and whole life.

Term Life Insurance

Term insurance is the simplest and cheapest form of life insurance because it pays only if death occurs during the term of the policy, which is usually from one to thirty years. Most term policies have no other benefit provisions. Term policies can offer (1) a level term, which means the death benefit stays the same throughout the term, or (2) a decreasing term, which means the death benefit declines, usually in one-year increments, over the course of the policy's term.

A form of term life insurance available to young parents is annually renewable term life insurance (ART). These term policies are renewable up to age eighty, but even though they cost less in the first few years, they cost more in the long run than the other term policies, particularly when prices rise annually. If you're in your early twenties and need to trim your insurance costs, you may want to buy a less-expensive ART for ten years and then switch to a thirty-year term policy down the road.

Whole Life Insurance

Whole life insurance creates a "cash value" that, if not paid out as a death benefit, can be borrowed or withdrawn on the owner's request. There are four major types of whole life or permanent life insurance:

- **Traditional Whole Life.** This policy provides stable premiums and death benefits. A whole life insurance policy covers you for your entire life, not just for a specific period such as term insurance. Your death benefit and premium in most cases will remain the same and builds cash value, which is a return on a portion of your premiums that the insurance company invests. Often, the insurance company will pay dividends if those investments grow. Also, if you opt out of the policy, you may receive what's left—once the cost of insurance has been deducted—but it's best not to rely on this as an investment strategy.

- **Universal Life.** This combines death protection with a savings account (sometimes known as the "cash value") that the insurer will invest in stocks, bonds, and money market mutual funds. The value of your policy may grow more quickly, but if the monies invested don't achieve profits, your cash value and death benefit may decrease. Some policies protect your death benefit from falling too far, but you need to read the fine print.

- **Variable Life.** This policy allows you to increase the death benefit, provided you pass a medical examination. The policy's premium dollars generally earn a money market rate of interest, and when you have sufficient funds (or "cash value") on hand, you may be able to use some of the cash value to lower your premium. Always check with your agent first to make sure enough funds are on hand to cover the premiums or you may risk losing your policy.

- **Variable Universal Life.** This policy is a combination of variable and universal life policies. It provides the investment risks and rewards of a variable policy, along with the ability to adjust your premiums and death benefits that comes with a universal policy.

Knowledge is Power ◄ Employers often subsidize their group insurance costs, so if your employer offers life insurance, it's worth exploring even if you have to contribute to it financially. Typically, groups are eligible for lower rates, the deduction comes out of your paycheck (possibly pre-tax), and you may be able to obtain higher coverage without health screening. Do compare the group rates with individual rates. Also keep in mind that if you carry more than $50,000 of group life insurance, the Internal Revenue Service (IRS) uses tables to determine how much it costs to provide the amount over $50,000 and charges you taxable income for that cost.

How Much Life Insurance Do I Need?

The Consumer Federation of America recommends that you buy eight times your annual income to cover living expenses for twenty years, or nine times for thirty years. If you want to cover college expense, add $100,000 per child. Then, deduct any life insurance provided by your employer.

Knowledge is Power ◄ If you are a single parent, be aware that, when you name your children as your life insurance beneficiaries, the proceeds do not have to go through probate and are not taxable as part of your estate. However, minor children cannot legally receive the proceeds. Make sure you assign a property guardian or custodian to receive and manage the funds until the children reach age eighteen—or an age that you, or your state laws, specify.

How Long Should I Carry It?

The longer the "term" (five, ten, fifteen, twenty, or thirty years), the higher the monthly premium. However, a thirty-year term may only cost an extra $12 to $15 per month, which is well worth it. If you're in your twenties and thirties and your children are toddlers, definitely opt for a thirty-year term. If you're in your forties and your children are in elementary school, the twenty-year term may be sufficient. Ideally, you want coverage until the wage earner reaches retirement, or until your children are earning a decent income. If you've invested well, your retirement fund should replace the need for life insurance upon retirement.

ONE-INCOME INQUIRY

What if I have a child with special needs?

If you have a child with special needs, you have special life insurance needs. You can still buy term insurance, but you'll want a policy that can be converted to a cash-value policy. This way you can keep a policy in place that protects your child for the rest of your life at a fixed cost.

How Much Does It Cost?

Insurance companies typically offer volume discounts—lower prices per $1,000 once you exceed a certain level of coverage. Price breaks usually occur in $250,000 increments. If you fall between breaks and can afford the higher cost, opt for the higher amount.

Prices can vary widely. The young and healthy win the lowest rates, but no matter your age, it's wise to comparison shop on the Internet. Be wary of sites that require your telephone number or employ agents who hard-sell cash-value or other life insurance options. Check sites such as *www.term4sale.com*, which compares 150 insurers to give you a concrete idea of the range of prices.

If your employer offers free, "portable" (so you can take it if you leave) or "convertible to cash" life insurance, take it and then supplement it with another policy if necessary. If the employer's life insurance isn't free, and you're relatively young, you may be able to find lower rates on your own. In all cases, research your options before signing on.

What If I Can't Make My Payments?

If you get in a bind and have trouble maintaining your premium payments, it can have immediate consequences. The effect depends on the type of policy and coverage you have and the policy terms and conditions. With term insurance, if you stop paying premiums, your coverage lapses. If you have whole life or universal life, you have several options:

- **Borrow Against Your Cash Savings.** You may be able to borrow, using your cash savings as collateral, or you may able to use your cash savings to cover the premium until you can get back on your feet. If you deplete the savings, you may lose the policy.
- **Forfeiture.** You can cash out the policy, but will no longer be covered by life insurance, and you may owe taxes on the portion of the cash value that exceeds what you have paid in premiums.
- **Non-forfeiture.** You may have a "reduced paid-up" option, which will allow you to stop paying premiums completely in return for a reduced death benefit and no cash savings. You may also be able to convert the permanent policy to an extended term policy for a time period based on the accumulated cash savings in the policy.

If you allow your whole life or variable life insurance policy to lapse, you may be able to reinstate it within five years of the lapse date. The insurance company will likely require a physical examination for the reinstated policy and you will have to pay back the premiums you would have paid, plus interest. However, your annual premiums for the reinstated policy may be lower than those for a new, comparable policy.

Disability Insurance Basics

Disability income insurance, which complements health insurance, safeguards your family in case the wage earner becomes sick or disabled. Even the healthiest among us can become disabled due to illness or injury. It has been estimated that 43 percent of all people above the age of forty will experience a long-term disability event by age sixty-five. They define long-term as lasting ninety days or more. When a one-income household is teetering on the edge and surviving month to month, a lot of bad things can happen in ninety days.

Basically, there are three type of disability insurance:

- **Employer-Paid Disability Insurance.** Many states require your employer to provide some form of disability insurance, but this may be limited to short-term sick leave. It's more common for larger employers to provide long-term disability coverage. This coverage usually pays up to 60 percent of your salary anywhere from five years to age sixty-five, and in some cases for life. Benefits from employer-paid policies are subject to income tax.

- **Social Security Disability (SSDI) Benefits.** These are funds that you (and your employer) have paid into through your social security payroll deductions and your employer's payments on your behalf. The requirements for benefit eligibility are considerable—your disability must be so severe that no gainful employment can be performed—and the benefits don't begin until five months after you've been injured or become ill. The amount the government pays is based on your average lifetime earnings, and you may have to pay taxes on your benefits. Generally, if you file a federal tax return as an "individual" and your "provisional income" (adjusted gross income, tax-exempt interest, and one half of SSDI benefits) is more than $25,000, you have to pay taxes. If you file a joint return, you may have to pay taxes if you and your spouse have a combined provisional income that is more than

$32,000. SSDI benefits are discussed in greater detail in Chapter 12, Mining Your Resources.

- **Individual Disability Income Insurance Policies.** These are policies you purchase on your own. Usually, those who purchase private policies are small business owners or people who are self-employed, but it's a great benefit to have if your employer does not provide adequate coverage. Private disability income policies typically replace 50 to 70 percent of your lost income. When you have paid the premiums yourself, these disability benefits are not taxed.

Insurers won't replace all your income because they want you to have an incentive to return to work. If your disability precludes a return to your usual profession, you are often eligible for retraining classes. It is important to pursue all your options and to take advantage of the protections in place.

If insurance is not available for the wage earner through his or her employment and you can afford extra coverage, having individual disability insurance is highly desirable. Particularly with one wage earner, the loss of income could devastate your family within a very short time. And, even if you are healthy, an accident could occur that leaves you partially or wholly disabled for a short time, a long time, or permanently.

While you may have some short-term state and long-term federal disability protection, it's wise to take advantage of additional disability insurance if your employer offers it. If you are solely responsible for your children, or if you earn a high salary, disability insurance is a worthy expense. Although disability insurance is essential for someone in a high-risk profession, anyone can quite suddenly become disabled. If you can afford it, buy it.

Buying Disability Insurance

If you have made the decision to buy disability insurance, start by talking to your insurance agent or agents—anyone who sells life, health, auto, or business insurance can likely steer you in a good direction. You can also log on to your state's insurance department website or call them for a list of agents and companies writing disability policies in your state.

Disability policies can be quite complex and quite expensive, so don't hesitate to ask your agent to clarify any terminology and clearly explain what you are buying. Disability premiums are based on your age, sex, occupation, and the amount of potential lost income you are trying to protect. If you are in a high-income bracket or in a high-risk profession, you'll pay more than someone who is not. Also, the higher the chance of injury, the bigger the premium will be. What you need to know:

- **How "disability" is defined.** Some policies pay benefits if you are unable to perform the customary duties of your own occupation; others pay only if you are unable to perform any job suitable for your education and experience; and some policies pay disability according to your own occupation for an initial period of two or three years, and then pay benefits only if you are unable to perform any occupation. " Own occupation" policies are more desirable, but also more expensive.
- **The defined benefit period.** The benefit period is the amount of time you will receive monthly benefits. Experts recommend benefits until at least age sixty-five, when social security disability will take over. If you are young, buying a policy with lifetime benefits may still be relatively inexpensive.
- **The percentage of income it replaces.** Policies may replace up to 60 or 70 percent of your total taxable earnings. Evaluate your other sources of income before deciding how much disability coverage you need.
- **The coverage.** Some offer an accident-only policy as an option. Although this can be less expensive, having both illness and accident coverage is preferable.

- **The waiting period.** Also known as the elimination period, this is the number of days you must be disabled before receiving benefits. If you are disabled during the elimination period, you will not receive any benefits, even though you are not able to work. If the elimination period is only thirty or sixty days, the premium will be higher. Most experts recommend sixty to ninety days. The first check is usually paid thirty days after the waiting period expires.
- **Whether there are cost-of-living adjustments.** If the policy doesn't provide cost-of-living adjustments, it may offer " indexed" benefits that provide inflationary adjustments after benefit payments begin.
- **Whether the policy includes residual or partial benefits.** If you're "partially disabled" you can perform some but not all of the major duties of your job or can only work part-time. Under a "residual" disability provision, you can receive a percentage of your disability benefit based on the percentage of income loss the sickness or injury has caused.
- **Whether the policy covers transition benefits.** Some policies offset financial loss while you rebuild a business or professional career during an additional disability insurance period.
- **Can they cancel?** A noncancelable policy will continue in force as long as the premiums are paid; neither the benefit nor the premium can change.
- **Is renewal guaranteed?** A guaranteed renewable policy will maintain the same benefits, but the insurer may be permitted to increase premiums for an entire class of policyholders that would include your job description.

Before you purchase a disability policy, be sure to research the company to make sure that it's financially secure. Your insurance agent or company representative should provide this information. You can also check the financial ratings of insurance companies with firms that verify this information. We have provided a list of such companies in Appendix C. You can also check with your state government's consumer affairs and business regulation department.

Saving Money on Disability Insurance

There are two ways you can lower your costs, but be sure to weigh the benefits against the long-term effects:

- Elect a longer waiting period before benefits begin. If you have enough resources to cover expenses during the first three months of disability, your premiums will be lower than they will be for coverage that starts after thirty days.
- Elect a shorter benefit period. Rather than benefits that cover the rest of your life, you can opt for benefits that end at age sixty or sixty-three. However, keep in mind that while this is very close to the age of sixty-five, when social security disability will begin, it's cutting corners right at an age when you may need the extra income.

Navigating Home, Car, and Mortgage Insurance

Chapter Ten

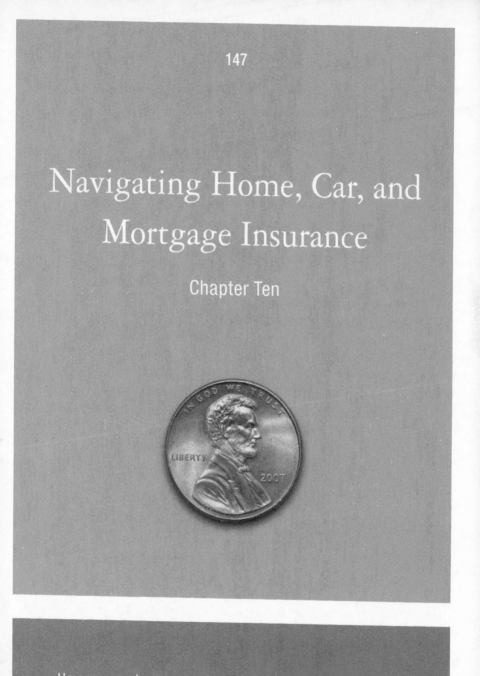

Homeowners Insurance • Mortgage Insurance • Automobile Insurance

ALTHOUGH INSURANCE CAN be costly, it is important to protect your assets and take measures to safeguard your ability to overcome disaster. This is especially important for a one-income household. Home, mortgage, and car insurance can be expensive, but it is not a place to drastically slash costs. Educated consumers want to secure their assets and protect their loved ones, without overpaying. Be sure to do your research before purchasing insurance. While insurance agents are knowledgeable and passionate about their profession, they are also salesmen who are trained to suggest multiple policies and maximum coverage.

Homeowners Insurance

Homeowners insurance typically covers the structure of your home, your personal belongings, your liability or legal responsibility for any injuries and property damage you or members of your family cause to other people, and displacement—living expenses if an insured disaster renders your house uninhabitable for a period of time. Most also cover damage caused by household pets. However, most policies do not cover maintenance problems (including damage caused by termites or mold), as the owners are responsible for maintaining the home and property.

The cost of your homeowners insurance will be based on the following:

- The square footage of your house and detached structures
- Replacement costs in your area, and any features that add to that expense
- The proximity and quality of fire service
- Your plumbing, heating, and electrical systems
- The risk of natural disasters, such as hurricanes, snowstorms, or hailstorms
- The crime rate in your neighborhood

Protecting the Structure of Your Home

Your insurance company will pay to repair or rebuild your home if it is damaged or destroyed by fire, hurricane, hail, lightning, or other disasters listed in your policy. Floods and earthquakes are not covered, so if you live in areas prone to either of these, you need a separate policy. If you live in a flood zone, you may be required to purchase flood insurance.

Knowledge is Power

Although earthquake insurance has become difficult to acquire, coverage may be available as an endorsement to your homeowners or renters policy. If not, your insurance company may offer a separate policy. The coverage typically kicks in after you pay a high deductible. In high-risk states, such as California, earthquake insurance may be available from the state. Check the California Earthquake Authority website (*http://earthquake authority.com*) for price and coverage comparisons.

Insured disasters typically include the following:

- Fire, smoke, and explosions
- Most natural disasters except flood, earthquake, landslide, mudslide, sinkhole, and others specified in your policy
- Lightning, windstorm, and hail
- Weight of snow, ice, or sleet
- Falling objects
- Theft and/or vandalism
- Accidental water or steam damage from plumbing, heating, air conditioners, sprinkler systems, or household appliances
- Damage caused by freezing of plumbing, heating, air conditioning, sprinkler systems, or appliances
- Sudden and accidental damage from artificially generated electrical current (with limitations)

- Damage by aircraft or vehicles
- Riots
- Volcanic eruption

ONE-INCOME INQUIRY

What does flood insurance cover?

Flood insurance typically covers the replacement cost for your home, but limits coverage for your personal belongings to their actual cash value, and may further limit coverage for furniture and other possessions stored in basements. Flood insurance is available for renters as well as homeowners. Even if you don't live in a designated flood zone, you might want coverage if your house is susceptible to melting snow, an overflowing creek, or water running down a steep hill.

When purchasing coverage for the structure of your home, it is important to buy enough to rebuild your home. The three types of structure coverage are as follows:

- **Actual Cash Value.** The policy covers replacement of your home or possessions, but will deduct depreciation.
- **Replacement Cost.** The policy pays the cost of rebuilding/repairing your home or replacing your possessions without deducting for depreciation.
- **Guaranteed or Extended Replacement Cost.** This option will pay whatever it costs to rebuild your home to its pre-disaster or pre-damage condition, even if doing so exceeds the policy limit. You may be covered for an additional 20 to 25 percent with this option. This is beneficial if you are in an area prone to natural disasters, where resultant material or labor shortages could spike prices. A guaranteed replacement cost policy may not be available if you own an older home.

Actual cash-value insurance may cost less, but can leave you underinsured. It's best to opt for a replacement-cost policy that doesn't subtract for depreciation and will cover the costs of rebuilding your house if it burns to the ground. If you want to save money, steer clear of "resale price" coverage, as this includes the value of your land, which is less likely to be severely damaged or devalued by fire or other disaster. Landscaping—trees, plants, and shrubs—is often covered under standard homeowners insurance, usually for 5 percent of the structure insurance. You will not be covered for damage by wind or disease. Most standard policies also include detached structures, such as a garage or tool shed, up to 10 percent of the structure coverage.

ONE-INCOME INQUIRY

How do I make sure I have adequate replacement coverage?
To ensure that you have adequate replacement coverage, multiply the total square footage of your home by local building costs per square foot. If you have no idea what that cost may be, you can get a reasonable estimate from a real estate agent familiar with the area and your style of home, or from a local builder, a builders' association, or your insurance agent. If you've upgraded your home, you'll want to factor that in. Plus, certain items increase replacement costs, such as fireplaces, custom cabinetry, hardwood floors, and marble countertops.

It is wise to review the face value of the policy annually to cover inflationary rebuilding costs, or to adjust for an increase in housing values. Ask your agent what you can do to bring the costs for "replacement-cost" policies down, such as installing smoke detectors, a fire extinguisher, or an alarm system.

Protecting Your Possessions

This portion of your policy covers furniture, clothes, and other personal items from insured disasters and theft. Coverage is typically 50 to 70 percent of the structure coverage. If you insure your home for $200,000, coverage for personal belongings would be somewhere between $100,000 and $140,000. Theft and damage coverage may extend off-premises, such as when you are traveling, although some policies limit this to 10 percent of your overall personal belongings coverage. Some policies even provide $500 in coverage for unauthorized use of your credit cards. Expensive furnishings and "luxury items" such as antiques, jewelry, furs, silverware, or art may only receive minimal coverage, such as $1,000 to $2,000 for everything. If you have such items, you may want to purchase a personal property endorsement or floater to cover their appraised value.

If you are renting a home or apartment, it's wise to buy renters insurance, which covers the costs of replacing your possessions in case of fire, damage, or theft. Save money by being realistic about values; what you think items are worth may be far more than their real value. What you want is sufficient coverage to be able to reconstruct your household in the case of a disaster or loss.

Liability Protection

Most policies provide no-fault medical coverage, which means that anyone (other than you or your family) who is injured on your property, or by your pets, can submit medical bills to your insurance company for $1,000 to $5,000. This helps avoid liability claims. If someone does file a claim, your liability coverage will pay for both the cost of defending you in court and any court awards—up to the limit of your policy. Liability limits generally start at about $100,000, but most agencies recommend a minimum of $300,000. If you have substantial assets that could be seized to settle a lawsuit, you may want to purchase an additional umbrella policy for $200 to $350 annually that will usually cover liability up to $1 million, including slander and libel.

Protection Against Displacement

This coverage pays hotel bills, restaurant meals, and other living expenses you incur if your house has been rendered uninhabitable—or has to be rebuilt—due to damages resulting from an insured disaster. Many policies cap coverage around 20 percent of the structure coverage. You can increase this coverage for an additional premium, but if you have relatives nearby that you can stay with until your home is repaired or rebuilt, you may feel safe trimming it back.

Saving Money on Homeowners Insurance

It is well worth your time and effort to seek ways to lower your homeowner's insurance costs. Often, you may be paying more than you really need to, and unless you're friends with your agent, the company isn't likely to review your policy annually to check for ways to reduce your premiums. It's up to you, as the homeowner (or renter), to make sure you have adequate coverage and are taking advantage of price-saving opportunities. Here are a few basic ways to lower your costs:

- **Compare Prices.** Experts recommend three price quotes. You can go online and compare prices easily. Begin with your state's government website where you will find a wealth of information by simply typing in "insurance price comparisons," or try comparison websites, such as *www.insure-net.com* or *www.insure.com*. These are usually more generic than the websites of individual companies.
- **Consult Independent Agents.** These agents often sell multiple policies or represent more than one insurance company. They are more likely to help you find the lowest-cost policy.
- **Think Outside the Box.** Professional or alumni organizations may offer discounts to members.
- **Deal with a Reputable Company.** You don't want to go so cheap that you are sacrificing adequate coverage. Make sure the company is legit and reliable.
- **Check the Company's References.** If you aren't familiar with the insurance company (or want to buy coverage online), check

its ratings or consumer complaint ratios. These will be available through your state government, the Better Business Bureau, or insurance watchdogs.

- **Buy from One Company.** If you buy your home and your automobile insurance from the same company, you will likely qualify for a discount between 5 and 15 percent. If you also buy an umbrella policy, the discount will likely be on the higher end.

- **Stick with the Same Company.** Some insurance companies reward long-term customers for their loyalty. Expect 5 percent for three to five years; 10 percent for six years or more.

- **Increase Your Deductible.** A jump from a $500 deductible to $1,000 may save as much as 25 percent on premiums. These days, most of us opt to pay for smaller repairs rather than boost our claims and risk a rise in premiums, making a $1,000 deductible a fairly safe gamble.

- **Install Fire and Theft Protection.** Most insurers offer discounts around 5 percent for smoke detectors, burglar alarms, or deadbolts. If you really fireproof with a sprinkler system and fire and burglar alarm that alerts the police and fire department, the company may trim your premium 15 to 20 percent. Be sure you ask first, as installing these systems can be pricey.

- **Disaster-proof Your Home.** If you live in a high-risk area, ask your agent what will lower the premium.

- **Ask about Discounts.** Discount opportunities may exist, but it's usually up to you to ask your agent if you qualify. If you're over fifty-five and retired, some agencies offer a 10 percent discount. Modernizing your appliances, your plumbing, or your electrical system also may lower your rates.

- **Review Your Policy Annually.** Do this both to make sure you have adequate coverage (replacement costs rise every year) and to make sure you aren't paying for items you no longer own.

Knowledge
is Power

Insurance companies are increasingly using your credit rating to judge prospective reliability and responsibility. Like it or not, they will compare your credit repayment habits with their best customers and make judgments about you that can raise or lower rates. If your credit rating is low, it's wise to clean it up before shopping for insurance. If it's stellar, use it as a bargaining tool for lower prices.

Mortgage Insurance

Basically, there are three kinds of mortgage insurance:

- **Mortgage Protection Insurance** is paid by the homeowner independently, or as part of the monthly mortgage payments. This insurance will pay the mortgage if the homeowner dies or is permanently incapacitated. In some cases, it also may cover payments if the homeowner is disabled or has temporarily lost his or her income.
- **Mortgage Indemnity Insurance** is insurance the lender purchases, although the homeowner pays for it either directly or indirectly. Mortgage indemnity insurance protects the lender if you're not able to pay your loan and they suffer a loss on the sale of the mortgaged home. However, it is important to understand that the insurance company will then attempt to recover the loss from the homeowner. Mortgage indemnity insurance is also known as lender's mortgage insurance.
- **Private Mortgage Insurance (PMI)** guarantees, in the event of a default, that the insurer will pay the mortgage lender for any loss resulting from a property foreclosure up to a specific amount. If a homeowner cannot pay 20 percent of the cost of the home as a down payment, the lender typically requires the borrower to purchase PMI. This protects the lender in case of fire or damage.

PMI doesn't cover the contents of your home, nor your equity. If you've reached the point at which your equity value is 20 percent of the value of the home, you should petition the lender to cancel PMI payments.

You don't need additional mortgage protection insurance if you have adequate disability insurance and sufficient life insurance to cover mortgage payments for the next ten to thirty years.

Automobile Insurance

Almost every state requires you to buy at least a minimum amount of liability coverage for your automobile—and minimums are usually not sufficient. ALL states have financial responsibility laws in place and it basically comes down to this: If you're found legally responsible for bills that are more than your insurance covers, you'll have to pay the difference out of your own pocket, which could easily create a financial disaster. If you are making payments on your car, your lender usually requires that you purchase comprehensive and collision insurance as part of the loan agreement.

Most states set standards for minimum automobile insurance coverage. Log on to your state's website or the Insurance Information Institute (*http://iii.org*) to find a list of minimum requirements for each state. There are certain areas where you can trim expenses; however, the best way to cut costs is to raise your deductible. For example, according to the Insurance Information Institute, increasing your deductible from $200 to $500 could reduce your collision and comprehensive coverage cost by 15 to 30 percent; raising your deductible to $1,000 can save you 40 percent, or more. Standard automobile insurance policies cover several areas.

Liability and Property Damage Coverage

At a minimum, you need bodily injury liability and property damage coverage. These cover injuries or damage you cause to other drivers, passengers, pedestrians, or property. Liability coverage usually specifies three numbers, such as 100/300/75. The Insurance Information Institute recommends that you carry these numbers as a minimum. The first number is the amount your insurance company will pay if one person is injured ($100,000); the second is the total amount it will pay if more than one person is injured ($300,000), and the third number is the maximum it will pay for property damage, such as damage to a fence, a house, a sign, a mailbox, and so on ($75,000). It's expensive coverage, but don't skimp, particularly if you have assets that an injured party could force you to sell to resolve a lawsuit.

Medical Payments or Personal Injury Protection (PIP)

This coverage will pay the medical expenses for the driver and passengers of your car(s). Since passengers are protected under your liability coverage, you may consider reducing or even opting out of this coverage if you have sufficient health insurance for yourself. Keep in mind, however, that PIP may also cover lost wages, the cost of replacing services normally performed by the person injured in an accident, and funeral costs.

Collision and Comprehensive

Collision covers the cost of damage to your car if you cause an accident, and comprehensive covers random damage or theft. Random coverage may include floods, earthquakes, storm or wind damage, or hitting a deer. States do not require that you carry collision and comprehensive, but lenders usually require coverage as part of the loan agreement. If your car is new, your loan agreement may require maximum coverage, but you can still opt for a high deductible. Collision coverage is generally sold with a deductible of $250 to $1,000—the higher your deductible, the lower your premium. For example, if you own your car and it's more than three years old, you may want to adjust the amount of collision and comprehensive downward, or opt out of it entirely, but keep in mind that the cost of repairs has risen dramatically. If your car is worth less than ten times the amount you are paying, you might want to drop this coverage.

ONE-INCOME INQUIRY

How Do I Determine the Value My Car?

As we all know, cars depreciate as soon as we drive them off the lot. Newer cars warrant higher coverage (and the lender will have requirements you must meet), but if you have an older automobile, it's wise to adhere to standard guidelines when determining its value for insurance purposes. You can find depreciated values for most cars in the Kelley Blue Book (*www.kbb.com*), or your insurance agent can refer to a National Automobile Dealers Association book (*www.nadaguides.com*).

Uninsured or Underinsured Motorist

This covers your expenses if an uninsured, underinsured, or hit-and-run motorist causes bodily injury to you or damages to your car. Leaving this out may or may not be fine. A majority of states provide uninsured motorist coverage by statute. Some states, however, require all automobile insurers to have uninsured motorist coverage in their liability policies. Other states only require automobile insurers to offer uninsured motorist coverage to their insured customers as an option to include in their automobile insurance packages. In these states, the insured can refuse to carry uninsured motorist coverage to reduce the cost of premiums. Individuals who choose not to include this coverage must typically rely on their own health insurance to cover personal injuries that result from car accidents. Check with your state's insurance agency (available online on your state's website) to see if it covers any of these costs.

If you are really strapped for cash and will find it difficult to make monthly car insurance payments, it still makes far more sense to raise your deductibles to keep premiums low than it does to minimize the levels of coverage. Your chances of not needing the coverage, and therefore not having to pay the high deductible, are greater than the chances of being able to pay tens of thousands or even more in the event of injury or property damage.

Umbrella or Extra Coverage

Most auto and homeowners policies have an upper limit on how much liability coverage they provide. If you have a lot of assets (above $300,000), or enough income to afford more coverage, you may want the extra protection of a personal liability or umbrella liability policy. These policies pay when your underlying insurance coverage has reached its maximum. Fortunately, they are reasonably priced, generally $200 to $300 for $1 million of coverage. If you use one company for both your homeowners and your automobile coverage, it may offer you the best price for an umbrella policy. If your automobile and home are covered by different agencies, it may be easier to buy umbrella coverage from your auto insurance company.

Minimizing Costs

If you have an excellent driving record, you may qualify for the lowest rates available. Amica offers low car insurance premiums to safe drivers, but you have to meet its rigid standards to qualify (*www .amica.com* or call 1-800-242-6422). Also, anyone with military experience, or who has a family member (parent or spouse) who served in the military, is eligible for reduced rates through USAA (*www.usaa .com*). Other ways to lower your rates include the following:

- **Drive safely.** Two moving violations in a year will raise your rates substantially for the next three years. Obtain a safe-driving pamphlet from your state's driver's license bureau, study it thoroughly, and abide by its laws. This may be available online; if not, you can write to your state's division of motor vehicles (DMV) to request one.

- **Contest traffic tickets.** Even if your culpability is indefensible, some DMVs—mostly due to budgeting limitations—will stop short of actually showing up in court. This means charges may be dropped, and you may be able to avoid those pricey points that boost insurance rates.

- **Pay all fines promptly.** The DMV has the right to suspend your license, which could cause you to lose your coverage, as well as spike your premium prices substantially for three years. Plus, failure to pay may be reported to credit reporting agencies, negatively affecting your credit rating.

- **Maintain good credit.** More and more insurance companies factor in your credit rating when determining rates. Studies have shown that drivers with solid, long-term, stable credit scores tend to be safer drivers, so if you have maintained a high credit score for a number of years, ask for a discount.

- **Take a defensive driving course.** You can save as much as 10 percent for three years.

- **Check your policy annually.** Benchmark birthdays can lower your rates. Young women's rates drop at age twenty-five. In some states, a young woman is considered an "adult" when she marries, and thus is eligible for lower rates even if she's younger than twenty-five.

- **Lower your mileage.** Mileage less than 5,000–7,000 miles per year earns lower rates.

- **Drive less-expensive cars.** Insurers base their rates on the car's sticker price (or its current resale value), the cost to repair it, its overall safety record, and the likelihood of theft. If your car is cheaper to repair and not particularly attractive to thieves, you may be eligible for lower rates. By all means, avoid SUVs. Companies will charge 5 to 20 percent more for SUV and sports car coverage.

- **Ask about discounts.** Being a nonsmoker, having a clean driving record, having automatic seat belts, and not using a cell phone in the car may qualify you for lower rates. Be sure to ask!

The following is a list of additional discounts that may be available, particularly if you shop around for the best rates:

- Insuring more than one car
- No accidents reported in the last three years
- No moving violations reported in the last three years
- Being a mature driver—over fifty-five years of age and retired
- Installation of an antitheft device (particularly if you live or work in urban areas)
- Having air bag protection, antilock brakes, and/or daytime running lights
- Student drivers who maintain academic excellence
- College students who are currently living elsewhere

Nonrenewal and Cancellation

If you fall behind on your insurance payments, the insurance agency may choose one of two options: cancellation or nonrenewal. If you have owned the policy for sixty days, the agency cannot cancel your policy unless the following has occurred:

- You have delinquent premium payments
- You misrepresented information on your application
- Your driver's license has been suspended or revoked

Insurance agencies can also opt for nonrenewal, which occurs when your policy expires. Generally, the agency must notify you prior to the expiration date and explain its reasons for failing to renew your policy. If this happens and it's due to something you have done or failed to do, you can contest the decision. If the matter is not handled to your satisfaction, you can file a complaint with your state's insurance department.

While cancellation may create hardships when it comes to securing a new policy—which invariably means higher premiums—nonrenewal usually doesn't affect what you will pay for new insurance.

Maximizing Tax Breaks

Chapter Eleven

Understanding Tax Basics • Tax Deductions for Homeowners • Child-Related Tax Credits • Timing Is Everything • How a Change in Marital Status Affects Your Tax Return • Filing Status • Avoiding Tax Errors • Tax Return Checklist • Avoiding Tax Scams

NO MATTER THE reason, or how slow or fast it occurs, when you find yourself in a situation where you transition from two incomes to one income, the last thing you want to do is pay any unnecessary taxes. Fortunately, you may well be eligible for credits and deductions that can help you. As a one-income household, you need to maximize any means of saving. Even if you love the government, you cannot afford to be one of its primary benefactors. After all, as an advertisement for Morgan Stanley (a financial investment firm) once touted, "You must pay taxes. But there's no law that says you gotta leave a tip."

Understanding Tax Basics

If you could minimize the amount of taxes you pay in a given year, wouldn't you jump at the chance? In fact, there are a number of legal methods you can use to minimize your federal income tax liability. It's incredibly important to know the basic rules and how to make the most of your tax planning opportunities. Maximizing all the deductions and tax credits you are entitled to—in the most efficient manner—is the key to saving big on your taxes!

Claiming Deductions

When preparing your tax return, you compute your gross income (salary, interest, dividends, alimony, disability payments, gambling winnings, tips and gratuities, canceled debt, and so on) and subtract certain deductions (IRA contributions, health insurance for the self-employed, moving expenses if related to changing job locations, and alimony paid) to arrive at your adjusted gross income (AGI). Next, you subtract other deductions, such as mortgage interest, real estate tax, medical and dental expenses, and contributions if you are using itemized deductions (or the standard deduction if you are not) and exemptions from your AGI to determine your taxable income. You use your taxable income to calculate your tax liability. Basically, it comes down to this: The higher your deduction level, the lower your tax liability.

Knowledge is Power

Many medical and dental expenses qualify for a tax deduction; however, you may be surprised at how inclusive they can be. Some that you might not expect include smoking cessation programs, acupuncture treatments, crutches, eyeglasses, and prescription drugs. To maximize medical and dental expenses, reference IRS Publication 502, *Medical and Dental Expenses*, which provides an authoritative list of eligible and nondeductible expenses.

To Itemize or Not to Itemize?

The next step is to decide whether it's more beneficial for you to take a standard deduction or to itemize your deductions. To determine this, calculate your tax return using both methods, and then select the one that gives you the lowest tax liability. The standard deduction is a fixed dollar amount, annually indexed (adjusted) for inflation, and is determined according to your filing status—such as married filing jointly or single—and certain circumstances, such as being head of household. Itemized deductions are various deductions that are reported on Schedule A of your federal tax return (Form 1040). These expenses include medical expenses, mortgage interest, state taxes, charitable contributions, theft losses, and other miscellaneous itemized deductions. If you have a number of deductible expenses, your itemized deductions will likely exceed your standard deduction. In that case, it would be to your advantage to itemize. Just be aware that there are some limitations regarding who can use the standard deduction and who can itemize.

Also, certain itemized deductions are available to you only if your expenses exceed a particular percentage of your AGI. For example, miscellaneous itemized deductions, such as employee expenses that were not reimbursed by your employer, gambling losses, union dues, and fees for safe-deposit boxes, are allowed only to the extent that they (when totaled) exceed 2 percent of your AGI. So, if your AGI is $100,000, your first $2,000 of miscellaneous itemized deductions won't count toward your total itemized deductions. Your medical expense deduction is also limited by 7.5 percent of your AGI. For example, if your qualifying medical expenses are $5,000 and your AGI is $60,000, then only $500 of your medical expenses will be deductible ($60,000 × 7.5 percent = $4,500; $5,000 minus $4,500 is $500).

ONE-INCOME INQUIRY

What if I make a lot of money?

If your income is too high, your itemized deductions may be limited. How high is too high? For 2008, itemized deductions were phased out when income exceeded $159,950 for single, married filing jointly, and head of household; $79,975 for married filing separately.

Tax Deductions for Homeowners

The IRS offers substantial tax deductions to compensate homeowners for defined expenses related to home ownership (because home ownership benefits our communities and our economy). These deductions apply whether you own a mobile home, a single-family residence, a townhouse, a condominium, or a cooperative apartment. To receive the tax deduction, taxpayers must itemize deductions on Schedule A of their tax return and file the IRS 1040 long form.

Mortgage Interest

Annually, your mortgage holder is required to mail you IRS Form 1098, listing the amount of the interest you paid for the full tax year. As we discussed in Chapter 6, the interest you pay for your mortgage loan can be claimed as an annual federal tax deduction based upon your marginal tax bracket. For instance, if you paid $15,000 in interest and your income placed you in the 15 percent tax bracket, you would save 15 percent of $15,000, or $2,250, in taxes. In this example your taxes would be $2,250 less when you claim the interest as a deduction. Not too shabby. Note: If your mortgage loan exceeds $1 million, the IRS imposes limitations on your deductible interest.

If you have a mortgage on a second home or an equity loan or equity line of credit on your primary residence, the interest you pay on those loans also is deductible. However, the amount you can deduct as interest is subject to certain limitations. The interest on a second or vacation home is generally deductible if you use the home as a residence for some portion of the taxable year, or if the interest satisfies the same requirements for deductibility as interest on a primary residence.

In fact, the second home does not have to be a house. It can be a boat or a recreational vehicle (RV), as long as it has cooking, sleeping, and bathroom facilities. For more information on mortgage interest, refer to IRS Publication 936, *Home Mortgage Interest Deduction*.

Real Estate Tax Deductions (property tax)

Homeowners also qualify for another major tax deduction based on their real estate or property taxes. If your property taxes are held in an escrow account controlled by your mortgage company, you will receive a statement (Form 1098) that specifies the amount you paid for that tax year. If you pay your property taxes separately, you will need copies of the tax bills and a record of your payments to compute your tax return.

Property taxes are deducted from your adjusted gross income. As with the mortgage interest, this is not a dollar-for-dollar credit. It reduces your tax by your tax rate percentage.

If you purchased a home in the current tax year, you are entitled to additional deductions. You can find the deductible expenses on the settlement sheet you signed at the real estate closing. Look for the terms "points," "loan origination fees," loan discount," or "discount points."

Getting a Tax Break When You Sell Your Home

When you sell your home, you are entitled to a significant tax break on your profit. This allows you to exclude up to $250,000 ($500,000 if married and filing jointly) of the gain (the price you paid for your home minus the cost basis) on the sale of your principal residence. Cost basis is the original amount that you paid for your home, plus purchase and selling costs, certain property renovations, and depreciation. The formula for calculating your cost basis on your main home is as follows:

>   Purchase price
> + Purchase costs (title & escrow fees, loan fees, and so on)
> + Improvements (replacing the roof, new furnace, new septic system, and so on)
> + Selling costs (staging costs, storage expense, real estate agent commissions, and so on)
> - Accumulated depreciation (for example, if you ever took the office in the home deduction)
> = Cost Basis

To qualify for the tax break on the sale of your personal home, you must meet the following qualifications:

- You have owned the residence for at least two years.
- You have lived in the home as your primary residence for at least two of the last five years.
- During the two-year period preceding the date of the sale, you have not excluded gain from the sale of another home.

In some cases, if you have owned and lived in your primary residence for less than two years and experience "unforeseen circumstances," you can still claim an exclusion. Unforeseen circumstances that force homeowners to sell before the requisite two years include:

- Death
- Divorce or legal separation
- Job loss that qualifies for unemployment compensation
- Employment changes that make it difficult for the homeowner to meet mortgage and basic living expenses
- Multiple births from the same pregnancy

If you have gone from two incomes to one income and suffer financial repercussions that force you to sell your home before you have lived in it for two years, this tax break can be very helpful in maximizing your profit. For more details, review IRS Publication 523, *Selling Your Home*, or consult with a tax specialist.

Child-Related Tax Credits

According to a report from the U.S. Department of Agriculture (USDA), it will cost a middle-income family with a child born in 2007 $204,060 to care for that child until his or her eighteenth birthday. For a middle-income, two-parent, two-child family, expenses for one child ranged from $10,930 to $12,030 per year, depending on the age of the child, with expenditures on teenagers being the highest. By comparison, the cost to raise a child to age eighteen in 1960 was $25,230, which would equate to $176,695, revealing that these costs have risen faster than inflation. However, there are several ways that your children can save you "tax cash" and lighten your burden a little. Let's consider the child tax credit, additional child tax credit, and child- and dependent-care tax credit.

Child Tax Credit

Your first savings is the child tax credit, for which you need no extra forms. However, you will need to meet certain tests and complete required worksheets before the IRS will let you take the credit.

If you have one or more qualifying children under the age of seventeen as of the last day of the tax year, you may be entitled to a credit of $1,000 per qualifying child through the year 2010. This amount is subject to a "phase-out" limitation based on modified adjusted gross income (AGI). For example, for 2007, the child tax credit began being phased out for modified AGI over $75,000 for single taxpayers; $110,000 for married individuals filing jointly; and $55,000 for married individuals filing separately. So basically, the credit is reduced by $50 for each $1,000 (approximately) of modified AGI over the threshold. In addition, the child tax credit is generally limited by the amount of the income tax you owe. For example, if the amount of tax you owe is $750 before the child tax credit, you would be entitled to only $750 of the $1,000 in child tax credit.

To qualify, your child (children) must meet the following five requirements:

1. **Age:** Was your dependent child under age seventeen at the end of the tax year (December 31)?
2. **Relationship:** Is the dependent child your son, daughter, adopted child, stepchild, eligible foster child, or your brother, sister, stepbrother, stepsister, or a descendant of any of these individuals?
3. **Citizenship:** Is the dependent child a U.S. citizen, a U.S. national, or a resident of the United States?
4. **Support:** Did the qualifying child NOT provide over half of his or her own support?
5. **Residence:** Did the qualifying child live with you? Each child must have lived with you for more than half of the tax year. (Note: Some exceptions exist; consult a tax specialist if necessary.)

According to IRS Publication 504, *Divorced or Separated Individuals*, divorced or separated parents have a special rule. In this situation, a child is treated as the qualifying child, or qualifying relative of his or her noncustodial parent, if all of the following apply:

- The parents (a) were divorced or legally separated under a decree of divorce or separate maintenance, (b) were separated under a written separation agreement; or (c) lived apart at all times during the last six months of the tax year.
- The child received over half of his or her support from the parents for the year.
- The child was in the custody of one or both parents for more than half the year.
- Either one of the following applied: (a) the custodial parent signed a written declaration that he or she will not claim the child as a dependent for the year, and the noncustodial parent attaches this written declaration with his or her return; or (b) a pre-1985 decree of divorce or separate maintenance or written separation agreement that applies to the given tax year states that the noncustodial parent provided at least $600 for the child's support during the tax year. If the decree of divorce was made after 1984, option (a) would apply.

Additional Child Tax Credit

Here's something you need to know: If the amount of your child tax credit is greater than the amount of income tax you owe, you may be able to claim some or all of the difference as an "additional" child tax credit. Yes, that means you can receive a refund even if you do not owe any tax. In recent years, the total amount of the child tax credit and any additional child tax credit was not permitted to exceed the maximum of $1,000 for each qualifying child.

To make sure you receive the appropriate child tax credits, follow the directions on IRS Form 1040 or 1040A and complete the child tax credit worksheet. You may also have to complete worksheets in IRS Publication 972, *Child Tax Credit*. If you qualify, use IRS Form 8812 to figure the additional child tax credit, and then attach it to your return. Note: You can find additional information and all of the IRS forms on *www.irs.gov*.

Timing Is Everything

Knowing your opportunities to use deductions and credits can help reduce your tax bill, but knowing how to time and report your deductions also can make a big difference. For example, most people report their income in the year that it's received, and report their deductions in the year that the expenses are paid. But what if you can control whether you incur the expense in this year or next?

Here's how it works: If you're in a higher income tax bracket this year than you expect to be in next year, you can accelerate your deductions into the current year to minimize your tax liability. You can do this by paying deductible expenses and making charitable contributions before year-end. For example, if you have major dental work scheduled for January of next year, reschedule it for December to take advantage of the deduction in the current year.

Here are some rules and tips you need to understand to take full advantage of timing:

- If you pay a deductible expense by check, make sure it's dated and mailed before year-end. However, it doesn't need to clear the bank by year-end.
- If you pay by credit card, the expense is deductible in the year the charge is incurred, not when the credit card bill is paid.
- A mere pledge or promise to make a charitable contribution is not deductible. Mail the check before the end of the desired tax year.
- If you pay estimated state income tax payments and need to lower your taxes in a high-income year, make the fourth-quarter

estimated state payment during the current year instead of the beginning of the next tax year.

- If buying a mutual fund in a taxable account, check when the fund makes its next distribution (similar to a dividend payment). Part of the distribution may be taxable, so if you buy just before a distribution you will have to immediately pay taxes on the fund's gains.

- Try to sell stock that you own after you've held it for at least a year; long-term capital gains rates are much lower than rates on short-term gains.

- If you have a gain in one stock and a loss on another, it may be worthwhile to sell both stocks so the gain on the first stock cancels out the loss on the second. This will eliminate the need to pay taxes on the gain.

Do you see how timing your expenses or your investments could help at the end of the year?

Knowledge is Power	◀	Along with your cash contributions to a charity, remember to deduct non-cash contributions, such as clothing, furniture, books, or whatever you donate. Ask for a receipt when you drop off donations. Also, you can deduct mileage (14 cents per mile for 2009) when you use your car for charitable purposes.

How a Change in Marital Status Affects Your Tax Return

Getting married, divorced, or losing your spouse are all extremely stressful events. The last thing you want to do is think about the negative effect the event might have on your tax return. Nevertheless, there are some actions you may want to consider that will be beneficial come tax time.

When marrying, be sure to promptly adjust the amount that your employer withholds for federal and state income tax from your paycheck by amending your Income Tax Withholding Form (W-4) to reflect your change in marital status and any change in the number of dependents. Your employer can provide this form. Typically, if you and your new spouse plan to file jointly, you probably want to boost the amount your employer withholds. Boosting your withholding may slightly increase your payroll deductions, but it will also ensure that you are paying enough taxes and preventing a huge tax bill come April 15.

If you are receiving alimony as a result of divorce, keep in mind that alimony is subject to federal and, in most cases, state income tax. Alimony also goes under the guise of spousal support, separate maintenance, or maintenance and support. You would be wise to plan for the extra tax by increasing your withholding on your tax return or making estimated tax payments.

If you are paying alimony, the amount you pay is deductible from your gross income. However, not all payments under a divorce or separation decree are considered alimony. Child support, non-cash property settlements, payments that constitute the spouse's or former spouse's share of community income, payments to maintain the payor's property when the spouse is living in the payor's property, and the use of that property are not considered alimony and thus are not deductible.

Filing Status

Whether you are single, married, or divorced, you may have filing status choices. Married filing jointly? Married filing separately? Single? Head of household? Which status do you pick? If you are legally married, you can choose married filing jointly or married filing separately. If you are not legally separated as of December 31 of a given tax year, you may elect to file a joint return for the year, even if you were living apart at the end of the year. If you have a legal separation agreement, you are considered unmarried and, therefore, must file as single (or head of household if you qualify). This may have advantages over married filing separately. The biggest difference when you file separately is this: if one spouse files using itemized deductions, the other spouse also has to itemize deductions, and vice versa. Married filing separately generally results in higher taxes than does filing a joint return. It is always a good idea to prepare your tax returns both ways, and then choose the filing status that results in the lowest combined tax.

If you are married and living apart from your spouse at the end of the year, you may elect the head of household filing status provided certain conditions are met.

Filing as Head of Household

If you are providing a home for your child, you are entitled to file as head of household. This entitles you to a lower tax rate and a higher standard deduction than if you filed single, or married filing separately. Qualifications that must be met include these:

- You have to be a U.S. citizen or "resident alien" for the entire tax year.
- You have to be unmarried or considered unmarried.
- You have to have paid more than half the cost of keeping up your child's home.
- Your child has to have lived with you for more than half the year.

To be considered unmarried for head of household purposes, you have to meet all the following criteria:

- You have to file a separate return.
- You have to have paid more than half the cost of keeping up your child's home for the tax year.

- Your spouse cannot live in the home during the last six months of the tax year.
- Your home had to be your child's principal home for more than half the tax year.
- You must be eligible to claim your child as a dependent. (This usually falls to the custodial parent, unless the child's other parent was given the right to claim the child.)

If you are the noncustodial parent, you can claim the child as a dependent if you meet *all* of the following requirements:

- You are divorced, legally separated, separated under a written separation agreement, or lived apart at all times during the last six months of the calendar year.
- You provide more than half of your child's support for the calendar year.
- Your child lives with you for more than half of the calendar year.
- The custodial parent makes a written declaration that he or she will not claim the exemption, and the noncustodial parent attaches the declaration to his or her tax return.

For more detailed information on divorce-related tax issues, consult IRS Publication 504, *Divorced or Separated Individuals.*

Filing as a Widow

If your spouse dies during the year, you are still permitted to file a joint return. For the two years after you filed a joint return with your deceased spouse—if you maintain the principal residence for your child or children—you may be able to file as a qualifying widow(er). This allows you to claim a standard deduction of $10,900 (for 2008), which equates to married filing a joint return. This is a savings of $5,450 over what you would have paid if you filed single, or a savings of $2,900 over what you would have paid if you filed head of household. This is assuming that you have not remarried.

ONE-INCOME INQUIRY

How can I maximize pre-tax dollars?

The government offers opportunities to use pre-tax dollars, but often it's only the rich who learn how to use them to their advantage. Two excellent ways to use pre-tax dollars are to fund IRAs that allow you to sock away money before paying taxes and that grow tax-deferred, and health savings accounts or flexible spending plans that use pre-tax dollars to pay medical expenses. Consult with a tax adviser or your company's benefits manager to take advantage of these tax savings.

Avoiding Tax Errors

It's impossible for you to know all of the tax laws, or how they have changed in recent years. You can review important information yourself, but it can be financially prudent to consult with a tax specialist, particularly if you think you're missing opportunities to lower your tax liability. Tax professionals can also make sure you don't make simple mistakes that delay your refund or lead to an audit. According to IRS Topic 303, *Checklist of Common Errors When Preparing Your Tax Return*, some of the most common errors are:

- Incorrect or missing social security numbers
- Incorrect tax entered from the tables
- Computation errors in figuring the child and dependent care credit or the earned income credit
- Missing or incorrect identification numbers for child care providers
- Withholding and estimated tax payments entered on the wrong line
- Math errors

Tax Return Checklist

Before you file your tax return, make sure you do everything in the following checklist to avoid holding up your refund:

- ❏ Did you enter the names and social security numbers for yourself, your spouse, your dependents, and qualifying children for earned income credit or child tax credit, exactly as they appear on the social security cards?
- ❏ Did you check only one filing status?
- ❏ Did you check the appropriate exemption boxes for all of the dependents claimed? Have you entered the total number of exemptions?
- ❏ If you are paper filing, as opposed to e-filing (Internet filing), do you have a Form W-2 from all of your employers, and did you attach Copy B of each to your return?
- ❏ If you owe taxes, did you enclose a check or money order with the return and write your social security number, tax form, and tax year on the check?
- ❏ If you are requesting direct deposit for a refund, did you provide the routing and account numbers?

❑ Did you make a copy of the signed return and all schedules for your records?

❑ Is the address on your return your most current address?

❑ If you are paper filing, did you mail your tax return to the government by certified mail with a return receipt requested? That is the only way that you can prove when you sent it and when the IRS received it. If the IRS loses your return, you have to prove that you sent it.

Avoiding Tax Scams

There have always been scam artists who thrive upon stealing your identity or who will rip you off via refund anticipation loans. The most common scams out there are phony refund e-mails, tax rebate scams, and fake audit announcements. It helps to always be skeptical and to know some basic facts.

For one, the IRS will *never* send you an e-mail to notify you of a tax refund. Unfortunately, some scam artists take advantage of anyone who doesn't know this simple fact by sending them an e-mail that has been designed to look like an official IRS e-mail. The e-mail typically notifies you that you are eligible for a tax refund of a specific amount or tells you that you are being audited and provides a link for you to fill out an electronic form. DO NOT click on this link. And never provide any of your private financial information, especially your social security number. The scam artist is phishing (using the Internet to fish for confidential information) for your personal and financial information. There have been cases in which taxpayers were called by scammers pretending to be IRS agents. To reel the taxpayers in, they offered a larger rebate for filing taxes early, and then requested bank account information, saying they needed it in order to deposit rebate checks electronically. Unfortunately, many taxpayers fell prey to this scam. DO NOT ever give any personal financial information to someone who calls YOU.

To protect yourself from scam artists, follow these basic rules:

- Never give out your personal and/or financial information over the phone.
- Never click on links provided in e-mails purporting to be from the IRS. If you receive an e-mail that claims to be from the IRS, ignore it, and contact the IRS by going to its website: *www.irs.gov*. If you want to know when your refund will arrive, access this information by clicking on "Where's My Refund?" on the real IRS website.
- Forward any suspicious e-mails to *phishing@irs.gov*.

Mining Your Resources

Chapter Twelve

Family and Medical Leave • Unemployment Benefits •
Disability • Workers' Compensation • Disaster Compensation
• Additional Government Assistance Programs • Cashing
In Life Insurance • Maintaining Your Health Insurance

IF YOUR FAMILY is forced to survive on one income, you may be eligible for federal, state, or local assistance. If the dip occurs suddenly due to illness or injury, you may be able to obtain immediate relief via unemployment, disability, or workers' compensation benefits. Other assistance may come in the form of veterans benefits, disaster relief, rental assistance, and food stamps. As a last-gasp strategy, you may be able to cash in your life insurance, and at the very least, maintain your health insurance at a lower cost. Whatever your situation, whether temporary or permanent, be sure to mine all of your available resources —they are there to serve you.

Family and Medical Leave

If you—or your spouse—needs to take time off from work to recover from an illness or to care for a family member, your rights are protected under the Family and Medical Leave Act. This act permits employees to take unpaid leave due to a serious health condition (one that makes the employee unable to perform his job), to care for a sick family member, or to care for a new child (birth, adoption, or foster care). The act also protects your right to return to the same position when the leave expires. If the same position is no longer available, your employer is required to offer you a position that is substantially equal in pay, benefits, and responsibility.

Fortunately, this helps many families during a difficult transition. Unfortunately, it's an unpaid leave, but it does offer you a reprieve if you have an emergency situation that requires you to take time off work. Leave is only available to those working for employers who have fifty or more employees within a seventy-five-mile radius. In addition, an employee must have worked for the company at least twelve months and worked at least 1,250 hours in those twelve months.

Unemployment Benefits

If you are laid off or lose your job due to no fault of your own, you are likely eligible for unemployment benefits—as long as you meet other eligibility requirements of state law. Basically, you must meet your state's requirements for wages earned or time worked during an established period of time referred to as a "base period." This typically means that you must have worked the first four out of the last five completed calendar quarters prior to the time when your claim is filed. Each state administers a separate unemployment insurance program within guidelines established by federal law. In the vast majority of states, benefit funding is based solely on a tax imposed on employers.

As soon as you become unemployed, contact your local unemployment insurance claims office. In some states, you are able to file a claim by telephone or over the Internet. It generally takes two to three weeks after you file your claim to receive your first benefit check. Some states require a one-week waiting period; therefore, the second week claimed is the first week of payment, if you're found to be eligible.

Once you have been approved and begin receiving benefits, you are required to file weekly or biweekly claims and respond to questions concerning your continued eligibility. You are required to report any earnings and any job offers or refusal of work during the week. These claims are usually filed by mail or telephone; your state will provide filing and continued eligibility instructions.

Some states require claimants to register with the state's employment service. Even if you are not required to register, this office can be a resource for finding a new job. The office staff will have information relating to the current labor market, and they often provide a wide array of re-employment services free of charge. They not only inform you of openings in your area, but will also advise you of available training programs. If nothing is available in your field, they may offer counseling and testing to help you discover new employment opportunities.

If you have special needs or considerations, such as physical limitations, that may prevent you from getting a new job, the state employment service will refer you to other agencies for help with those needs.

In general, benefits are based on a percentage of an individual's earnings over a recent fifty-two-week period until it reaches the state's maximum amount. Benefits can be paid for a maximum of twenty-six weeks in most states. Some states only pay benefits for thirteen weeks, but you may be eligible for an additional thirteen weeks through federal unemployment. During times of high unemployment, some states provide additional benefits. Benefits are subject to federal income taxes and must be reported on your federal income tax return. You may elect to have the tax withheld by the state unemployment insurance agency.

Disability

Should you or your spouse become ill or injured, there are three alternative sources of income replacement:

- **Employer-paid Disability Insurance.** Check with your employer immediately to verify your coverage. This coverage usually pays up to 60 percent of your salary anywhere from five years up to age sixty-five, and in some cases for life, dependent upon the nature of the disability and the provisions of the policy.
- **Social Security Disability Benefits (SSDI).** SSDI benefits are paid to people who cannot work because they have a medical condition that's expected to last at least one year or result in death. Federal law requires this very strict definition of disability. While some government programs give money to people with partial disability or short-term disability, social security does not. The requirements for eligibility are consid-

erable—your disability must be so severe that no gainful employment can be performed. If your application is approved, your first SSDI benefits do not begin until five months have passed. Your first payment comes at the end of the sixth full month.

- **Individual Disability Income Insurance Policies.** If you have a private policy, call your agent to verify the benefits.

Federal Disability

The Social Security Administration (SSA) administers two programs that provide benefits based on disability: the Social Security Disability Insurance (SSDI) Program and the Supplemental Security Income (SSI) Program. SSDI provides for the payment of disability benefits to individuals who pay the social security tax on their earnings, as well as to certain dependents of insured individuals. SSI provides payments to individuals (including children under age eighteen) who are disabled and have limited income and resources. We will limit our discussion to SSDI, which is most relevant to a family that has lost a wage-earner's income due to disability.

ONE-INCOME INQUIRY

How Much Will I Receive from SSDI?

The amount of your monthly SSDI disability benefit is based on your average lifetime earnings. The Social Security Statement that you receive each year displays your lifetime earnings and provides an estimate of your disability benefit. It also includes estimates of retirement and survivors' benefits that you or your family may be eligible to receive in the future. If you do not have your Social Security Statement and would like an estimate of your disability benefit, you can request one at *http://socialsecurity.gov* or by calling (800) 772-1213.

Under SSDI, individuals who can qualify for benefits on the basis of disability include:

- A disabled insured worker under the age of sixty-five
- A person disabled since childhood (before age twenty-two) who is a dependent of a deceased insured parent or a parent entitled to Title II disability or retirement benefits
- A disabled widow or widower, age sixty-two or older, if the deceased spouse was insured under social security
- Your spouse at any age if he or she is caring for a child of yours who is younger than age sixteen or disabled
- Your unmarried child, including an adopted child, or, in some cases, a stepchild or grandchild, if he or she is under age eighteen, or under age nineteen if in elementary or secondary school full-time
- Your unmarried child, age eighteen or older, if he or she has a disability that started before age twenty-two and meets the definition of disability for adults

While some programs give money to people with partial disability or short-term disability, SSDI does not.

WHEN DO SSDI BENEFITS BEGIN?

By law, SSDI for workers and widows usually cannot begin until five months after the established onset of the disability. The five-month waiting period does not apply to individuals filing as children of workers.

A few states offer State Disability Insurance (SDI) that will assist you while you are awaiting final approval. Five states currently offering SDI are California, Hawaii, New Jersey, New York, and Rhode Island.

WILL I BE ELIGIBLE FOR MEDICARE OR MEDICAID?

When you are receiving SSDI, you may also be eligible for Medicare, which can help pay hospital and doctor bills. It generally covers:

- Anyone sixty-five and over
- Anyone who has been determined to be disabled and has been receiving benefits for at least twenty-four months
- Anyone who has amyotrophic lateral sclerosis
- Anyone who needs long-term dialysis treatment for chronic kidney disease or requires a kidney transplant

In general, Medicare pays 80 percent of reasonable charges.

The government automatically enrolls you in Medicare after you receive disability benefits for two years (from the date you were entitled to receive disability, not the month you received your first check). Medicare has two parts: hospital insurance and medical insurance. Hospital insurance helps pay hospital bills and provides some follow-up care. The taxes you paid while you were working finances this coverage, so it's premium-free. The medical insurance portion helps pay doctors' bills and other services, but you'll have to pay a monthly premium.

In most states, individuals who qualify for Supplemental Security Income (SSI) benefits based on financial need also qualify for Medicaid, which will cover all of the approved charges for the Medicaid patient. Although federal and state governments finance Medicaid or other similar programs, eligibility rules may vary from state to state.

CAN I WORK AND STILL RECEIVE DISABILITY BENEFITS?

If you're working and your earnings average more than $940 a month (in 2008), you generally cannot be considered disabled. If you have been classified as disabled and are receiving disability benefits, you may be able to work while continuing to receive benefits. In fact, Social Security encourages claimants to test their ability to work and permits them to do so without losing their rights to cash benefits and Medicare or Medicaid. These rules are called "work incentives." The rules are different for SSDI and SSI, but both programs provide:

- Continued cash benefits
- Continued help with medical bills
- Help with work expenses
- Vocational training

For more information about work incentives, ask any social security office for *The Red Book—A Guide to Work Incentives* or visit *www.ssa.gov/redbook*.

HOW DO I APPLY FOR SOCIAL SECURITY DISABILITY (SSDI)?

You can apply for disability benefits online at *www.socialsecurity.gov* or go to your local social security office or call (800) 772-1213 to make an appointment to file a disability claim over the telephone. Once you schedule an appointment, SSA will mail you a Disability Starter Kit to help you prepare for your disability claims interview, which will last for roughly one hour. You will need to have the following information ready:

- Your social security number and date of birth
- The amount you earned last year and how much you expect to earn this year (and next year, too, if you apply between September and December)
- Information about your illnesses, injuries, and current condition, plus contact information for your medical care providers
- The name and address of each employer for the last two years
- Your last Social Security Statement (review it first for inaccuracies)
- Name, social security number, and date of birth of your current spouse and any former spouse(s), plus marriage and divorce information
- Names of your dependent natural children, adopted children, stepchildren, and grandchildren (if they live with you) who are under age eighteen, or any child disabled before age twenty-two.

You can speed up the review process by providing the following information when you submit your formal application:

- A copy of your birth certificate, or proof of original citizenship or naturalization
- Names, addresses, and phone numbers of the doctors, caseworkers, hospitals, and clinics that provided care, and the dates of your visits
- Names and dosage of all prescribed medicine
- Any medical records from your doctors, therapists, hospitals, clinics, and caseworkers that you already have in your possession
- Any laboratory and test results you may have on hand
- A summary of your work history and a description of your duties
- A copy of your most recent W-2 form (Wage and Tax Statement) or, if you are self-employed, your federal tax return for the past year

In addition to the basic application, you will need to fill out additional forms. One form collects information about your medical condition and how it affects your ability to work. Other forms allow doctors, hospitals, and other health care professionals to send the government information about your medical condition.

Employer Disability

Hopefully, your employer offers disability insurance. Failing that, most are required to offer a short-term sick leave, which could range from a few days to six months. State laws in Hawaii, New Jersey, New York, and Rhode Island require employers to offer disability benefits for up to twenty-six weeks. However, there are no laws that require employers to offer long-term disability (LTD) coverage.

If you work for a large or mid-sized company, you may be one of the lucky ones with employer-paid disability insurance. If that's the case, and you become sick or disabled, immediately alert your benefits department and ask the following questions:

- How much will I receive?
- How long until the benefits kick in?
- How long will I receive benefits if I remain disabled?
- Does the employer's disability plan take other disability programs, such as social security, into account when calculating my disability pay?
- Am I responsible for any tax payments on the income?

Typical group long-term disability benefits replace about 60 percent of the worker's usual salary. These benefits usually start when short-term benefits are exhausted and continue from five years up to life. Usually, group long-term disability insurance is fully paid for by employers, and you are required to pay federal and state income tax on the benefits, unless paying these taxes on your behalf is another benefit your employer provides.

Workers' Compensation

If you are injured while working, or if your illness was caused by your employment, you may be eligible for workers' compensation. Workers' compensation may be paid by federal or state workers' compensation agencies, employers, or insurance companies on behalf of employers.

If you are receiving public disability payments—social security benefits, civil service disability benefits, military disability benefits, state temporary disability benefits, or state or local government retirement benefits—your monthly disability benefits will be added together with your workers' compensation. If the total amount of these benefits exceeds 80 percent of your average current earnings, the excess amount is deducted from your social security benefit. If your employer has a human resources manager, contact that person immediately to obtain information, file a claim, and gain immediate access to available benefits. If your company does not have a human resources manager, or if you are self-employed, contact your state's Department of Labor to acquire information and file a claim. The telephone number and address will be listed in your phone book, or you can log on to *www.dol.gov* for more information.

If you were injured in an automobile accident, your car insurance or the car insurance of the person who caused the accident may cover you.

Disaster Compensation

If your area is affected by a disaster, you may be eligible for low-interest disaster loans via the U.S. Small Business Administration (SBA) to cover uninsured property losses. Loans are available for repair or replacement of homes, automobiles, clothing, or other damaged personal property. Loans are also available to businesses for property loss and economic injury.

Additional assistance is often available from the Federal Emergency Management Agency (FEMA) when the president declares a major disaster as the result of a hurricane, earthquake, flood, tornado, or major fire. This money comes from the President's Disaster Relief Fund, managed by FEMA, and other federal disaster aid programs or grants. FEMA may offer disaster relief as follows (after insurance coverage has been exhausted):

- **Temporary housing:** Money is available to rent a place to live, or to pay for a government-provided housing unit when rental properties are not available.
- **House repair:** Money is available to homeowners to repair damage caused by a disaster to their primary residence above that which is covered by insurance. The goal is to make the damaged

home safe, sanitary, and functional. FEMA does not pay to restore your home to its previous condition.

- **Replacement:** Money is available to homeowners to replace a home destroyed in a disaster not covered by insurance.
- **Permanent housing construction:** Direct assistance or money for the construction of a home is usually only available in insular areas or remote locations specified by FEMA, where no other type of housing assistance is possible.

Further assistance for needs beyond housing may include:

- Disaster-related medical and dental costs
- Disaster-related funeral and burial costs
- Clothing; household items (room furnishings, appliances); tools (specialized or protective clothing and equipment) required for your job; necessary educational materials (computers, schoolbooks, supplies)
- Fuels for primary heating source (heating oil, gas)
- Clean-up items (wet/dry vacuum, dehumidifier)
- Repair of disaster-damaged vehicles
- Moving and storage expenses related to the disaster (moving and storing property to avoid additional disaster damage while repairs are being made to the home)
- Other necessary expenses or serious needs as determined by FEMA

Immediately after the president's declaration of a disaster, federal disaster workers arrive as soon as possible and set up a central FEMA field office to coordinate the recovery effort. They typically publish a toll-free telephone number for affected residents and business owners to access information. Disaster Recovery Centers also are opened, where disaster victims can meet with program representatives and obtain information about available aid and the recovery process.

Disaster Unemployment Assistance

The Disaster Unemployment Assistance (DUA) program provides unemployment benefits and re-employment services to individuals who become unemployed due to major disasters. Benefits begin with the date the individual became unemployed due to the disaster and can extend up to twenty-six weeks after the presidential declaration date. These benefits are made available to individuals not covered by other unemployment compensation programs, including self-employed individuals, farmers, migrant, and seasonal workers.

All unemployed individuals must register with the state's employment services office before they can receive DUA benefits. Most states have a provision that an individual must be able and available to accept employment opportunities, but not all states require an individual to search for work.

Legal Services

When the president declares a disaster, FEMA, through an agreement with the Young Lawyers Division of the American Bar Association, often provides free legal assistance to disaster victims for cases that will not produce a fee. If you need assistance, ask FEMA if you can receive free legal consultation. The assistance typically includes:

- Help with insurance claims (life, medical, property, and so on)
- Counseling on landlord/tenant problems
- Help dealing with consumer protection matters, remedies, and procedures
- Replacement of wills and other important legal documents destroyed in a major disaster

Special Tax Considerations

Taxpayers who have sustained a casualty loss from a declared disaster may deduct that loss on the federal income tax return for the year in which the casualty actually occurred, or elect to deduct the loss on the tax return for the preceding tax year. A casualty loss can result from the damage, destruction, or loss of your property from any sudden, unexpected, and unusual event such as a flood, hurricane, tornado, fire, earthquake, or even volcanic eruption. In order to deduct a casualty loss, the amount of the loss must exceed 10 percent of the adjusted gross income for the tax year by at least $100.

The Internal Revenue Service (IRS) can expedite refunds to any taxpayers living in a federally declared disaster area. An expedited refund can be a relatively quick source of cash, does not need to be re-paid, and does not need an Individual Assistance declaration. Log on to the IRS website at *www.irs.gov/taxtopics/tc507.html* for additional information.

Additional Government Assistance Programs

If you have fallen below the poverty line, you're not alone. According to the Sargent Shriver National Center on Poverty Law (2008), the latest poverty statistics are as follows:

- 12.9 million children, which is four times the number of all the children in Illinois
- 3.6 million seniors over sixty-five, equal to the entire population of Oklahoma
- 14.6 million women, equal to the combined populations of Wisconsin, Indiana, and Iowa
- 8.0 million disabled, a population larger than the state of Massachusetts
- 3.5 million homeless, equal to twice the population of Nebraska

If you're in the same boat as these millions of Americans, the online Catalog of Federal Domestic Assistance (*www.cfda.gov*) provides access to a database of all the federal programs available. You can use the database to find assistance programs that meet your requirements and for which you are eligible. Once you have targeted agencies, contact the office that administers the program and ask how you can apply.

ONE-INCOME INQUIRY

What if I Am a Veteran?

If you are a veteran, or your spouse is, you are eligible for many federal programs that offer assistance, including pensions, low-cost housing loans, health insurance, vocational rehabilitation, life insurance, and survivors' benefits, among others. Log on to *www.va.gov* for more information, or call your local department of veteran affairs.

Rental Assistance

If your income is severely limited, the Department of Housing and Urban Development (HUD) provides housing assistance to approximately 1.5 million American households through three basic programs:

1. **Public Housing.** HUD provides subsidized rental housing for low-income families, the elderly, and disabled individuals in everything from single family houses to high-rise apartments. Though funded by the federal government, assistance is handled by local city or county agencies. Renters pay reduced rates, with the amount determined by their gross income, minus deductions.
2. **Vouchers.** The renter finds his own privately owned apartment or rental house, and HUD provides vouchers or certificates to cover all or a portion of the rent. The housing has to meet HUD requirements for safety and health. Vouchers are also managed by local city or county agencies.
3. **Subsidized Housing.** These funds are paid directly to the property owners, who then apply the funds to cover rents from approved low-income renters.

These benefits are typically available to families whose income does not exceed 50 percent of the median income for the area (adjusted for smaller and larger families) and, on an exception basis, those whose income does not exceed 80 percent of the median income for the area (adjusted for smaller and larger families). At least 75 percent of families admitted to the voucher program must be extremely low-income families—those whose income does not exceed 30 percent of the median income for the area. To find out the median income for your area, log on to *http://huduser.org/datasets/il/FY2008index_mfi.html.*

HUD also protects both renters and property owners. Renters are required to make their monthly rent payment on time, maintain the property, and abide by the terms of the lease. Owners are required to provide safe and sanitary housing, make timely repairs, respect the renter's privacy, and refrain from discriminatory practices.

Details on all HUD programs are available at *www.hud.gov.* If you are interested in applying for public housing, contact your local housing authority. This will be listed in your phone book's government pages.

Food Stamps

Depending upon your income, the number of your dependents, applicable deductions, and your available resources, you may be eligible for a number of Child and Adult Care Food programs, including food stamps. The government helps 26 million low-income and needy families afford nutritional food each month. To find a complete list of government programs available, and to determine your eligibility, log onto *www.fns.usda.gov* or contact your local food stamp office. Other programs available to low-income families include the following:

- **The Child and Adult Care Food Program (CACFP)** provides meals and snacks to children and adults who receive care in nonresidential day care centers. CACFP reaches even further to provide meals to children residing in homeless shelters, and snacks and suppers to youths participating in eligible afterschool programs.

- **The Commodity Supplemental Food Program (CSFP)** works to improve the health of low-income pregnant and breastfeeding women, other new mothers up to one year postpartum, infants, children up to age six, and elderly people at least sixty years of age by supplementing their diets with nutritious U.S. Department of Agriculture (USDA) commodity foods.
- **The Farmers Market Nutrition Program (FMNP)** provides fresh, locally grown fruits and vegetables from farmers' markets to eligible women, infants, and children. Seniors may also be eligible for savings coupons.
- **The National School Lunch Program (NSLP)** helps school districts and independent schools that choose to take part in the lunch program get cash subsidies and donated commodities from the USDA for each meal they serve. In return, they must offer to eligible children free or reduced-price lunches that meet federal requirements. Summer Food Services are also available through various activity programs.
- **The School Breakfast Program (SBP)** operates in the same manner as the National School Lunch Program, serving free or reduced-price breakfasts to eligible children.

Assistance for Seniors

If you are retired and your social security payments are not meeting your expenses, you can seek financial help from a variety of government programs including SSI, food stamps, and Medicaid. Medicaid provides medical coverage to those who can no longer afford care. Often it doesn't kick in until all your assets have been depleted, but there are some protections in place for your family. Although it's a federal program, state governments administer the program. Phone numbers will be available in the front of your local telephone book, or you can log on to your state government's website for more information.

Other possibilities include the following programs and services, which are offered by the government or by charitable organizations:

- Meals on Wheels
- Adult day care
- Assistance with energy bills
- Transportation assistance
- Subsidized housing
- Property tax rebates

If you are a senior citizen and need financial assistance, explore all of your options, and don't feel shy about applying—you've earned it.

Cashing In Life Insurance

If you have term insurance, you won't have any equity in your policy to cash in, and if you cancel the policy, you will no longer have coverage. However, if you have a whole life, universal life, variable life, or a variable/universal life policy, you may have accrued cash value—the amount of money that you accrued above the cost of the insurance or that has grown due to investments—and may be able to tap into the savings to either reduce your premium or to borrow from the savings. Please review the section on life insurance in Chapter 9 before making any decisions. Keep in mind that your agent may tout the virtues, but gambling with your life insurance during difficult financial times may cause unnecessary stress. If you have small children or other dependents, surrendering life insurance can jeopardize their security. Always check with your agent first to understand the full consequences.

Maintaining Your Health Insurance

If you lose your employment, and your employer provided your family's health insurance, there are usually two options available that will protect your family.

- **The Consolidated Omnibus Budget Reconciliation Act (COBRA)** requires employers who employ more than twenty workers to offer continued health insurance coverage to employees who are fired or who leave for any reason. You can opt to continue health coverage at the employer's costs, plus 2 percent, for a period of eighteen months. Legally separated, divorced, or widowed spouses are eligible for thirty-six months of coverage via COBRA. However, you must accept the offer within sixty days (thirty days if your spouse died). Don't wait! COBRA protects you, and your children, during transitions, and it's highly doubtful that you'll be able to find independent coverage at less cost.
- **The Health Insurance Portability and Accountability Act (HIPAA)** protects your access to health insurance. Under HIPAA, those who leave a group insurance plan are guaranteed coverage as long as they were covered for at least twelve months and switch health care providers within sixty-three days.

One of the smartest things you can do is take advantage of COBRA and HIPAA to ensure that your family will not be turned down, or made to wait for coverage. Allowing a break in insurance gives insurance companies the opportunity to deny coverage, or withhold specific coverage on the basis of pre-existing conditions.

Living Frugally

Chapter Thirteen

Creating a New Dream • What You Need to Know about
Warehouse Stores • What to Buy at Discount Stores • Save
on Groceries • Trim Energy Costs • Avoid Guzzling Gas •
Have Fun Without Spending Money

FRUGALITY IS ITS own reward. Although it seems like the antithesis of what the American culture preaches, frugality and living within—or ideally below—one's means can feel fantastic. Although we are bombarded with advertising, the truth is that all those gadgets, fancy cars, expensive clothing, and jewelry are not what bring ultimate happiness. The "good life" won't look quite so good if you're lying awake at night worrying about foreclosure, or if you're slaving away daily to make enough to sustain exorbitant car payments and pay down bulging credit card balances. Feeling secure, safe, and comfortable will bring you far greater happiness than this false sense of wealth. And, as we'll discuss toward the end of this chapter, having little money to spend can actually bring families closer together, if only because you have to find ways to entertain yourself and your children that don't cost money. Many of these activities will actually foster genuine and invaluable interaction.

Creating a New Dream

We've all grown up feeling entitled to the American Dream and all the goodies that come with it, and it's hard to shake the idea that accumulating possessions is desirable. Who doesn't grow up wanting a great house in a great neighborhood, or the financial wherewithal to buy two cars, cushy furniture, and a big-screen TV? The problem is that few of us can really afford what was once the American Dream.

What you need is a new dream, one in which you use your ingenuity to create ways to save money. The thrill will come when you realize how easy it becomes to substitute shopping and spending with creativity and pride. Instead of limping home from a shopping spree already feeling the letdown, you'll come home feeling proud that you've either resisted spending unnecessary money or found a creative way to spend a lot less. Hopefully, this will lead you to the real nirvana—living and thriving within your means.

What You Need to Know about Warehouse Stores

The oversized warehouse stores—such as Sam's Club, BJ's, and Cost-co—may or may not provide bargains. Without a doubt, you can make some stellar buys, but it's important to check the unit pricing. Since most of these stores sell goods in extremely large packages and don't provide unit pricing, you'll need to conduct your own research by bringing along a calculator. If you know the unit prices you typically pay, you can determine whether or not you're getting a bargain.

There are definite drawbacks to these mega-stores, as well. You also have to add in the cost of the annual fee ($25–$35), and keep in mind that they often don't honor coupons and don't mark down items to attract customers. Also, you invariably end up buying items you don't need, spending far more than you would at your local grocery. To check out a store's viability, purchase a one-day pass (usually available for $5 to $10 with a small surcharge added to your purchase). Go armed with your calculator and later compare their unit prices with your grocery store prices. If the bargains are worth it, go once a month and restrict buying to the highly discounted products. While there, ask yourself firmly, "Can I live without this?" If the answer is "no," and you can stick to buying only what you need and what is truly a bargain, then by all means buy the items. To save on your costs, you could also go shopping with a friend and co-buy items that you split.

Knowledge is Power ◄ Many grocery stores offer a "customer card" free of charge. For some grocery chains, these have replaced store coupons, and are always worth having, as you may see your total cost drop significantly as your card computes the discounts. Some drugstores, such as CVS, also offer customer cards that provide "instant rebates" in the form of coupons printed with your receipt. Take full advantage and you may save $20 to $40 a month.

What to Buy at Discount Stores

There are definitely certain items that are worth the trip to a discount store. These include:

- **Cleaning supplies.** Although the proximity of the cleaning supply aisles at the grocery store seems too convenient to ignore (which is what they count on), cleaning supplies can usually be purchased at discount stores for 20 to 40 percent less than the grocery store price. Sunday magazine circulars typically feature cleaning supply coupons that discount stores such as Kmart or Walgreen's will honor. To really save on cleaning supplies—and be fashionably "green"—use a simple mixture of white vinegar and water, or baking soda and water, for most cleaning needs.
- **Paper products.** Wholesale clubs and discount stores frequently have lower unit costs on paper towels, bath tissue, and other paper products. You have to buy in bulk, but this is one area where the savings are worth the trip.
- **Pet food.** You may pay as much as 35 percent more when you buy pet food at your local grocery store. Check out pet stores, where the variety and prices are often better, or research the unit price at discount and warehouse stores.

Use the Internet as an Ally

The Internet has opened up vast opportunities to save money. If you're a Net surfer, you can easily find websites that offer coupons, discounts, and bargains. Establish a free e-mail account and use it exclusively for online bartering. Sample clubs (try Startsampling.com, Olay.com, or Eversave.com) will send you free samples of products in exchange for an occasional marketing survey. Other online clubs (Momdotcom.net, Thefrugalshopper.com, Mycoupons.com, or Justfreestuff.com) offer free samples of a variety of products, and often sponsor contests that award money or prizes.

You can also use the Internet to comparison-shop for goods and services (Bizrate.com, Pricescan.com, or Epinons.com) and find the lowest price online. Often you can print out the page and use it to barter with a local store, which means you get what you want at the lowest price, and you save on shipping! Also you can locate coupons (Couponmaker.com, Siteforsavings.com, Couponnet.com, or Valpak. com) that you can print and take to a local retailer.

Many online retailers offer codes that you enter to save money or obtain free shipping. Individual retailers usually have information listed on their websites, but you can find a variety of codes by visiting code or code forum sites (Slickdeals.com, Jumpondeals.com, Edeals. com, Fatwallet.com, or Dealcatcher.com). Many also offer point programs (Mypoints.com, Cafemom.com, or Ebates.com) in which you accumulate points that add up to savings.

Save on Groceries

Groceries are, unfortunately, becoming so high priced that we all have to take a step back and reassess how we allocate the money we spend on food and other products purchased at the grocery store. Rather than panicking and lopping off food items, sit down and review your buying habits and preferences to create a workable plan. There are, of course, certain simple steps you can take to spend less on food and other grocery store products.

Create a Pantry

Even if your house doesn't have a pantry, consider creating a space where you can store bulk items, such as canned or dried foods, and other sale items that will store safely for long periods of time. You could adapt a small closet or set up shelves in your basement. Even an attic space will work, in the winter, or if it is air-conditioned. The idea is to scan the sales flyers and stock up when items you use regularly have an attractive price, and preferably a coupon that lowers the price even more. This way, you can maximize savings and have a full pantry that helps you resist impulse buys. Once the pantry is full, it's often easier to find something to make right at home, saving a trip to the store or takeout place to put dinner on the table.

Knowledge is Power	Don't buy packages of grated cheese. Buy cheese in bulk, grate it yourself, and store multiple bags in your freezer. Ditto for pre-mixed salads. It's far cheaper to buy a few types of lettuce, a variety of raw vegetables, and bag your own salad mix. Wash the lettuce and vegetables, spin the lettuce in a salad spinner to dry it, then store everything in plastic bags or containers until you're ready to mix up a salad. Again, this saves money, and is better for you!

Stock Up Your Freezer

If you don't have a freezer, investigate the cost of buying a small one. Contrary to popular belief, it's doesn't cost that much to keep an extra freezer in your basement or garage (probably less than $10 a month). Then, just as you'll stock your pantry with sale items, you can stock your freezer with whatever meats or fish are on sale. Be sure to write the date purchased on the freezer bag so you can use the oldest items first. This also helps you avoid impulse buys, save money, and plan meals ahead of time.

Always Shop with a List

We all know the value of this guideline, but the vast majority of us go to the market without a list. By making a list and sticking to it, you can save hundreds of dollars each year in impulse buys. Besides, once you've familiarized yourself with the cheapest prices, you'll know when and where to look for foods that you repeatedly buy.

Consider yourself a shopping warrior—a heroic figure who maintains sharp focus on the job at hand and doesn't allow herself or himself to be diverted by glossy advertisements, dangling sale signs, or other temptations to buy things you don't really need. Be the warrior who fights the battle at hand, triumphantly leaving the market with the list fulfilled and your checkbook strengthened.

Knowledge is Power	Don't buy boxed pre-seasoned rice and pasta—they cost more than plain rice. Buy low-sodium bouillon cubes instead and add them to the water you cook the rice in for added flavor. You can also throw in a generous dash of your favorite herbs and spices, and add a teaspoon of olive oil or butter. Your rice will taste great, save you money, and be better for you!

Use Coupons

According to Stephanie Nelson, of Couponmom.com, over $318 billion worth of grocery coupons are distributed each year, and 99 percent of those coupons are thrown away. Nelson notes that the cost of groceries constitutes the third-highest expense in the average household's budget, and recommends saving big by using coupons. "By combining sales with coupons, it is possible for many households to cut their grocery bills in half. I believe that [most people toss the coupons] because they are tedious and time-consuming to use." These days there are many websites offering coupons for virtually everything you need. You select and print only the coupons that will actually save you money on your grocery bill.

Also, keep in mind that stores will frequently honor other stores' coupons. Often you can use drugstore coupons at your local grocery store. Since drugstores often provide a steep discount, and most grocery stores now have their own pharmacies, you can save quite a bit by taking time to peruse the circulars. Also, some retailers offer to match the lowest prices you can find, and some stores will double or even triple coupons. Be sure to go the service desk and ask about your favorite store's policies—it may just save you a bundle.

Knowledge is Power ◀ When you see a sign that offers "twenty for $10" realize that you don't typically have to buy twenty items to get the discount. Stores generally price the items individually, in which case you pay fifty cents per item no matter how many you buy.

Nelson also recommends that you grab a copy of the store's sale flyer as you enter the store. These ads are usually in a rack near the entrance. By quickly scanning the front and back pages, you may find sale items that you need.

Knowledge is Power ◀ Now that many grocers are offering rotisserie chicken, you can often find the day-old ones on sale for half price. They may look a bit shriveled, but the chicken is still tender and delicious. When you buy these chickens, use every last bit of meat, and then toss the bones into a pot to make broth. You can buy other marked-down meats as well.

Don't Dawdle

The more time you spend meandering through the aisles, the more you spend. Both for health and monetary benefits, try limiting yourself to the perimeters of the market, where the fresh vegetables, fruits, meats, fish, bread, and milk are found, and skipping the bakery, the cookie aisle, the snack aisles, and the soda aisles. It's interesting to note how easy this becomes, and how much you save by realizing that you don't need anything down those aisles. Since you'll be buying canned goods when they go on sale, you can safely venture down those aisles with your list tightly gripped in your sweaty palm. Select only what you need, and make a mad dash to the cash register!

Be Creative

When it comes to beauty products, a little Dove (or any other unscented, pH-balanced) soap goes a long way. Add a little cornmeal, oatmeal, or sugar to exfoliate. You can also skip the fancy creams and use baby oil, olive oil, or even Vaseline or Crisco to lock in moisture. Tepid or cold (never hot!) wet tea bags placed over swollen eyes work miracles. A homemade mixture of one egg yolk, two tablespoons of plain yogurt, and a teaspoon of honey will serve as a great mask. Watered-down lemon juice or witch hazel will serve admirably as an astringent. Instead of expensive eye creams, pierce a vitamin E capsule and dab the oil lightly around your eyes and mouth. Baby shampoo is cheap compared to regular shampoo, and mayonnaise makes a great hair conditioner. You can also safely water down your expensive shampoo and conditioner by 25 to 50 percent and not affect their performance!

Buy Generic

This goes for everything from aspirin to tomato sauce. Most of us either buy the brands our mothers bought or what we've seen ads touting as the best product. The truth is that generic products or store brands are often just as good as the national brands, and are made with virtually identical ingredients. In fact, the same plant that packages brand names often packages generic, store-branded items using the very same, or similar, food product. Most grocery chains have rigorous standards for their store-branded food products, requiring that they be as good, or better, than the leading national brand. When you buy brand-name products, you are paying for their advertising, packaging, and reserved places on grocery store shelves. A Gallup poll once revealed that somewhere between 84 and 90 percent of us buy name-brand products.

Savings from buying store brands can range from 15 to 30 percent, so it's a great way to trim your weekly grocery bill.

You can also:

- Buy staples, such as canned goods, salad dressing, mayonnaise, and so on, at a discount store (offers sharp discounts, two for the price of one, etc.).
- Avoid prepackaged or frozen goods.
- Check your receipts for errors before you leave the store.
- Buy cosmetics at discount drugstores (cheaper than grocery stores).
- Plant a vegetable garden, or buy at farmers' markets just before they close.
- Never shop hungry (following just this one step will save you 10 percent a year).
- Shop on Monday (prices are usually lower).

Trim Energy Costs

Unfortunately, energy costs are spiraling out of control—out of *our* control, anyway. We can't control the prices, but we can control our consumption. There are a multitude of things you can do that will make a difference. If you don't see changes happening immediately, don't lose heart; these small steps will begin to add up. Hopefully, you'll also lobby for progress, by advocating higher miles-per-gallon (mpg) standards for automobiles, solar energy, and a variety of "green" transformations that can ultimately affect our entire nation. Meanwhile, here are ideas on what you can do to decrease your energy consumption.

Minimize Laundry Expenses

There are several tips to doing laundry that can save money. First and foremost, use an Energy Star washing machine and dryer. If you don't already have these, or can't afford to buy them now, make sure that energy efficiency is high on your list the next time you do buy. They can vastly reduce the amount of water used (by as much as half), as well as clip energy costs by as much as 35 to 50 percent. Other tips include these:

- Wash only full loads whenever possible. Don't overfill the machine, however, as that sometimes means you have to go back and wash clothes that didn't quite come clean.
- Unless clothing is unduly soiled, wash almost everything in cold water. If you need warm water to fully clean soiled laundry, opt for warm rather than hot, and always finish with a cold rinse. Some believe liquid detergent works best for cold-water washes.
- Use only as much detergent as you need. It's wise to check the recommended amounts and make sure you're not using too much detergent. Not only is that bad for your budget, it can leave a film on your clothes. If the clothes are barely soiled, you can usually use less than the recommended amount of detergent. Manufacturers are now touting "concentrated" detergents, and changing the size of dispensers, so it's smart to double-check them often.
- Buy store brand or less expensive detergents. Avoid all the bells and whistles, because few of them make any difference. Instead of buying expensive spot sprays, try the old-fashioned soap-and-scrub method. Or, dab the spot with a white vinegar and baking soda paste or with lemon juice (if the garment is white). Wash your delicates in ordinary dish soap—if it's gentle enough for your hands, it's gentle enough for your hand-washables.
- Don't overdry clothes. Consider hanging them outside to dry; not only will your laundry smell clean and fresh, you'll save money.
- Limit the purchase of clothes that require dry-cleaning.

Use Appliances Efficiently

You can trim your energy costs by taking a few simple steps to improve appliance efficiency. For instance, don't preheat an oven unless your dish will bake in less than an hour, or unless you are baking bread, cookies, cakes, and so on. Use a toaster oven or microwave whenever possible. Other steps you can take include these:

- Set the thermostat on your water heater at 120° F. If you'll be away for a week or more, turn it even lower. This can save you as much as 50 percent on the heating costs.
- Buy and install an insulated water heater cover and save 15 percent.
- Check with your local energy provider to find the ideal off-peak hours. The cheapest time to use appliances may be in the early morning or late evening, dependent upon where you are. Running your washing machine, dryer, and dishwasher during these times may save you a lot of energy costs over the long run.
- Replace incandescent light bulbs with compact fluorescent bulbs. They use 75 percent less energy and last ten times as long.
- Ask your electric and gas providers for an audit of your energy use. They will often perform these free of charge.
- Log on to *http://homeenergysaver.lbl.gov* and fill out the questionnaire, which will tell you how much energy you're using and how you can cut expenses.
- Take shorter showers. Showering for three to five minutes rather than ten to fifteen minutes may cut your energy bill by as much as 30 percent, and trim your water bill too.
- Add weather stripping to plug up any areas where air seeps in or out.
- Use the sun as an ally. In winter open your drapes at daylight, and close them at night.
- Avoid wide fluctuations in temperature. It's good to lower your thermostat at night, but moving the regulator up and down er-

ratically can increase energy costs. In winter, dress in layers and nuzzle under blankets; in summer, open the windows and use a fan—and be willing to sweat occasionally.

If you have difficulty getting your children to understand that leaving lights on or running their computers or televisions night and day runs up your electric bill, make a deal with them. Divvy up the electric bill, and tell them they will each receive a certain amount of money, but they have to use a portion of it to pay their share of the electric bill. If the bill exceeds their allotted amount, they will have to make up the difference with their regular allowance. This creates a win-win situation, as they'll soon realize that some bad habits (the ones Mom was always nagging them about) erode their pocketbooks. Most kids will soon begin snapping off the lights and limiting the amount of time they use energy. This way they'll learn how to take responsibility for everyday bills and how to conserve energy. If they take excessively long showers, you may want to divvy up the water bill too.

Avoid Guzzling Gas

Over the years the cost of gas has skyrocketed. It's now more important than ever to adopt gas-saving habits—in your car and at home.

First and foremost, when it comes to your car, drive a fuel-efficient model. Rarely will it be possible to thrive on one income if you have a gas-guzzling SUV—or two! You may not be able to trade your car for a new hybrid, but if you have two cars and are paring down to one, shop around to see if you can find an inexpensive new or used model. If you own SUVs or other gas-guzzling mega-mobiles, it may save you quite a bit if you trade one, or both, for one fuel-efficient model.

You can also try to live with one car and take public transportation whenever possible, particularly if you're commuting into a city and spending massive amounts of time in long lines of traffic. All that maddening stop and go eats up the gas—and your soul. Taking public transportation or carpooling will save not only gas, but also tolls and parking expenses. Better yet, if you are lucky enough to be in a situation that allows you to work online, perhaps your employer would be willing to let you work from a remote location—your comfortable home—a few days a week.

To save as much as possible on gas, try these ideas:

- Make sure your car is serviced regularly, and keep your tires fully inflated.
- Use cruise control on the freeways. This keeps your highway time safer, steady, and legal, and you conserve gas.
- Buy regular unleaded rather than premium gas. According to experts, there's little to no difference in the quality, and virtually no difference in requirements for the vast majority of cars. Double-check your owners' manual to be sure.
- Research your area to find out which gas station consistently offers the cheapest prices. You can do this by calling around or asking friends. Also, check out GasBuddy.com and GasPriceWatch.com. Even during times of wildly fluctuating prices, you can usually find one or two stations that consistently offer low prices.
- Fill up on Tuesday or Wednesday, when prices dip slightly. Weekends typically bring the highest rates. Try to avoid buying gas on major holiday weekends.
- Join up with fellow parents to carpool kids to and from activities and/or school.

Have Fun Without Spending Money

Even though you want to save money in your new one-income life, you still want to enjoy yourself. Well, you don't need money to have fun. In fact, once you open the door to new ways to entertain yourself and your children, you'll be surprised at how much fun you'll have and how easy it is to find quality entertainment for a dime. Use your ingenuity, and that of your children, to come up with a long list of activities you could do separately, and as a family, that cost little or no money. Not only will your children participate, they'll love the game—and they'll learn that it is possible to have a great deal of fun without breaking the bank.

Knowledge is Power ◀	Volunteering is a great way to lift your spirits. Habitat for Humanity, for example, may offer opportunities for the whole family to team up with neighbors to build houses for the underprivileged. You can also team up to help a local charity raise money for afterschool programs or summer camps, or national organizations to support research programs to combat cancer or other illnesses. Instead of feeling deprived, channel your energy into productive activities—it will give your spirits a boost while saving you hundreds of dollars!

Entertaining Children on a Dime

Entertaining your children doesn't have to cost money. Instead of relying on television or video games, everyone will benefit if you find other, inexpensive ways to amuse your kids.

How about a few ideas that involve art? Team up with your children to create a creativity box or basket. Toss in paints, scissors, decoupage paste, buttons, paints, rhinestones, beads, glitter, confetti, pressed leaves or flowers, magazines, ribbons, string, wrapping paper, shells, unwanted promotional CDs (compact discs, that is!), broken toy bits, keys, and other odds and ends—basically whatever you and your children can think of that might be fun to use. On rainy days try some of the following creative activities:

- Buy an inexpensive birdhouse (check your local hobby store) or use a small box to create a birdhouse, and then paint or decoupage it.

- Decoupage magazine art onto poster board to create personal collages.
- Use discarded keys to make a wind chime.
- Paint or paste things onto those unwanted promotional CDs and use them to create a mobile.
- Spend the day weaving string friendship bracelets. String a few beads onto them or weave in ribbons for variety.
- Buy blank note cards or stationery from the hobby store's dirt-cheap bin (or at a dollar store) and teach your children the value and beauty of handmade gifts, note cards, and gift tags by letting them create some for their friends and family.

You can also spend a day gardening with your children. It will be a form of cheap entertainment, a learning experience, and fun for all. A few days prior, sit down with a gardening magazine or book (which you can get at the library) and use its help to pick out flowers and plants that you and your children would like to grow. Take your kids to the hardware or discount store to buy the materials you'll need. If you're planting small cuttings or seeds, have the children decorate small clay pots or containers. Then, spend a day sowing seeds or planting cuttings.

One of the best ways to save money when you have children to entertain is to take advantage of your local libraries. You can borrow not only books, but also CDs and videos. Most libraries also offer storytelling sessions and special events, including making crafts or exploring living history, all of which are free.

Rather than feeling deprived, think of these "free activities" as golden opportunities to introduce your children to the luxury of doing nothing. They will cherish the memories of chasing butterflies or fireflies, running through the sprinkler, climbing trees, picking fresh berries, playing hopscotch, fielding baseballs, creating treasure maps, stacking cards, inventing words, making finger puppets, lying on their backs gazing at clouds or stars, playing kick the can, eating watermelon and seeing who can spit the seeds the farthest, creating a fort out of cardboard boxes, playing dress-up and creating a play (including jerry-rigging props), hiking through a forest, wading through streams, creating a puppet show, telling stories around a campfire, catching frogs and letting them go again, or pretending they are explorers and going on a treasure hunt. When it comes to entertaining, educating, and enriching your children, use your imagination instead of your wallet. Each of these activities is fantastically fun for children, and they'll love you for sharing your imagination and what they consider your most precious asset—yourself.

Here are a few more ideas to try:

- Go on picnics. Pack their favorite snacks, as well as some games to play. Include nature studies, such as bird watching or guessing the names of flowers, plants, or trees. (Check out free nature guides from your local library.) Try a nighttime picnic and include stargazing.
- Attend a local ballgame. If you live close to an inexpensive minor league park, you can spend far less money and still enjoy all the raucous fun. If you don't live close to a ballpark, perhaps a college, high school, or local league plays regularly nearby.
- Take them to local music, dance, or theater performances.
- Play board games. Despite the popularity of video games, there's nothing like old-fashioned board games. Children love them and love having the undivided attention of their parents.
- Play active games. You can usually lure even a sullen teenager outside to play catch or shoot hoops. Younger children would enjoy hopscotch, kick the can, or hide-and-seek. You can also try badminton, roller-skating, or bike riding.
- Invite their friends over for sleepovers and have them create their own pizzas, pop their own popcorn, or bake their own brownies.
- Spend Saturdays or Sundays exploring the world around you. Places such as historic sites; state or local parks or gardens; scenic

areas such as rivers, lakes, or ponds; or ethnic areas such as Little Italy or Chinatown can all offer their own thrills.

Here's your basic assignment: Instead of spending money, spend time dreaming up ways to enjoy life. Get as crazy and creative as possible, and have your children come up with their own lists. You'll teach them how to entertain themselves and to enjoy the world around them—valuable lessons indeed!

Free Entertainment for Adults

Get yourself a pad of paper and go online to find a ton of ideas. Log on to websites of the surrounding communities and make a list of all the free activities you can find that might interest you. For instance, in the Cape Cod area you can watch cranberries being harvested and processed; watch glassmaking at the oldest existing glasswork business; brush up on marine biology at the Woods Hole Oceanographic Institution; take a self-guided tour of the Cape Cod Lavender Farm in Harwich; take a free tour of the Chatham Lighthouse; watch boats race and sailors compete in various regattas throughout the summer in Buzzards Bay; or catch a Cape Cod Baseball League game and get a sneak peek at upcoming major league stars. You'll be able to find activities like these near your home as well.

Your own community is also likely to have a number of free activities that you and your family can enjoy. To find out about what's going on in your own neighborhood, check out the following:

- Stop by your local city hall offices and ask for a community calendar, which lists year-round events—everything from free concerts to parades.
- Stop by your local parks and recreation department to find a list of parks, hiking trails, classes, and events offered in your community.

- Stop by your library to find a list of book clubs and events, such as art openings, lectures, or other library-related events.
- Look for a community bulletin board where people post upcoming events or social opportunities, such as bird-watching clubs, garden clubs, social clubs, charity events, or antiques fairs.
- Subscribe to your local paper.

A treasure trove of free events and entertainment is also available online. Find lists of free things to do in cities across the country at *www.free-attractions.com*. Find links to sites where you can find free entertainment at *www.coolfreebielinks.com*. And look for free downloads of classic books, such as the complete works of authors including Shakespeare, Jane Austen, and Charles Dickens, at *www.gutenberg.org*.

You can also create your own excitement at home. Consider these ideas:

- Start a card club or bridge club and invite your friends to bring their favorite dish.
- Start a hobby club in which each member hosts a night at his or her house to share a unique talent, such as decoupage, beading, knitting, gardening, cooking, woodworking, lure making, model railroading, and so on.
- Have an old-fashioned treasure hunt at a flea market.
- Spend a Saturday checking out local recycling centers where small shops house free castoffs.
- Start your own book club, wine tasting club, gardening club, or cigar club.
- Invite your friends over for a spa night, including manicures, pedicures, facials, and gossip.

Other Fun Ways to Live a Fantastic Frugal Life

Shop vintage stores! In recent years, vintage and consignment stores have grown in popularity because they often hold treasures at very affordable prices and because browsing in them is fun. Even if you don't find a bargain, rummaging around often provides a virtual walk down memory lane. The same applies to antiques stores or fairs— as long as you set a minimal budget and spend most of your time window-shopping for amusement. Outdoor fairs can provide a full day's entertainment, as long as you resist the urge to buy big-ticket items, like furniture—unless you really, really need it *and* it fits into your budget. You can occasionally indulge a fascination with antique postcards, inexpensive jewelry, teacups, or whatever gives you a cheap thrill. Flea markets are another way to shop without spending much. Auctions are also fun, but only when you're shopping for affordable treasures—old picture frames, a silver cake knife, an antique watch, or a vintage hat—or using it as a learning experience. If you go to auctions, determine what you can afford to spend for each item before you start bidding and stay within those parameters. Remember, no matter where you shop, there's nothing wrong with just looking.

Museums and art galleries are another source of inexpensive entertainment—and education. Most museums offer a free day every month or week, and many have discounted prices during off-peak hours.

Basically, it comes down to this: There are concrete steps you can take to trim your budget in fairly significant ways, and doing so will bolster your family's financial base, bring you closer together, and often benefit the environment. Rather than mindlessly doing the same things you have always done, embrace the value in thinking outside the box and adopting new habits, places, and ideas. Once you begin, you're not only likely to see instant results, but will experience the thrill that comes with saving—rather than constantly spending—money.

Blindsided: What to Do When Disaster Strikes

Appendix A

Crisis Management in a Box • Picking Up the Pieces
• Calculating Your Income • Calculating Your Expenses •
Making Smart, Necessary, Immediate Decisions •
Negotiating Payments • Staying Afloat

AS WE ALL know, disaster can strike at any time. And since the vast majority of us are living paycheck to paycheck, the loss of one paycheck can quickly spiral you into a crisis situation. Ideally, you would have planned for that possibility and had an emergency fund in place, but realistically, we know it's unlikely that most people have sufficient funds on hand. If you are thrown into a crisis situation, the following sections will help you cope with the issues at hand. Once you've got a secure handle on the crisis, you can then methodically go through the rest of the book to make long-term decisions that will bolster your financial stability.

Crisis Management in a Box

Disasters come in all shapes and sizes, but the most familiar financial disaster occurs when one member of a two-paycheck family loses his or her job unexpectedly. This could come in the guise of a short- or long-term layoff, the loss of job through abrupt dismissal, or an illness or accident that renders one unable to work. We all sail along on a wing and a prayer, but accidents happen—and we are all susceptible. If you're lucky, you've had an inkling that danger is ahead, but all too frequently this happens with no prior warning. One day you and your partner are gainfully employed and meeting all of your financial commitments; the next day someone has been laid off, fired, in an accident, or disabled. If you don't have an emergency plan in place—and funded—you'll find yourself in a crisis situation and in desperate need of crisis management.

Knowledge
is Power

"The two-income family is like a speeding racecar.
It goes faster than its one-income counterpart, but if
it hits a rock, it careens out of control and crashes."
Elizabeth Warren, author of *The Two-Income Trap*.

A crisis situation demands a crisis mentality. There is no time for denying what's really happening, or procrastinating. If your family plunges from one income to two, you must take the financial reins immediately and create a survival plan. We'll give you twelve hours for wailing, bemoaning, cursing, and grieving, but there's no time to wallow. Wishing and hoping your situation will change is unproductive. What you need is a plan.

Picking Up the Pieces

Again, your first response will be to panic. It is a crisis situation, and a mélange of unfavorable feelings—disbelief, anger, panic, and fear—are bound to occur. It is important to acknowledge those feelings, but the best remedy for panic is to get a firm grip on your new reality. Even if you think you know every nook and cranny of your finances, it's extremely important that you sit down with your partner, pen and paper in hand, and assess exactly where you are financially now—today—this instant! To begin, answer the following questions:

- **Is this likely to be a short- or long-term situation?** If you can realistically determine that the second income will be revived or replaced quickly, it greatly affects your chosen course of action. A quick replacement may mean a short-term tightening that you can weather; a long-term situation most likely means that you will have to take immediate action to drastically cut your living expenses. It is important throughout this process to be realistic. If one is going to err, then err on the side of expecting the worst (while hoping for the best).
- **Will the person who lost his or her income be eligible for unemployment insurance?** If the person who lost his or her job is eligible for unemployment insurance, go to the U.S. Department of Labor website (*www.doleta.gov*). This site provides basic information and links to your state government site for the specifics that apply to your situation. It can also help you determine exactly what you can expect as income, and the length of time the unemployment benefits will apply. Use this figure to compute the

budget you'll need to weather this storm. If you don't have access
to a computer, look for your state offices in the yellow pages and
visit them in person.

- **If there was an accident, was it work related, making you
eligible for workers' compensation?** If your accident occurred
while you were working or is in any way work related, you will
most likely be eligible for workers' compensation. Your company's human resources director should help you file the necessary
paperwork immediately.

- **Do you have disability insurance that will cover a portion of
the lost income?** If you are disabled due to illness or an accident
and have disability insurance either through your employer or on
your own, determine exactly how much income you can expect
to receive and the length of time it will be provided.

- **Do you have mortgage or credit card insurance that will
cover lost income?** If you opted for mortgage insurance that
covers illness or unemployment, find the policy and determine
how much it will cover and the length of time this expense will
be covered. Also, if you have credit card or other debt insurance,
determine what will be covered, and for how long. Often credit
card insurance will cover your minimum payments throughout
the course of the illness.

- **Do you have an emergency fund or savings account, and if
so, how much is currently on hand?** Ideally, you'll have savings or an official "emergency fund" that you can call upon. Find
the most recent statement and write down exactly how much you
have on hand.

- **Do you have liquid assets you can cash in?** If you have liquid
assets, such as a savings account, stock, bonds, cars, boats, or
expensive household items that you could sell to generate cash,
estimate the likely income.

- **Do you have a retirement fund?** If you have a retirement fund,
you may consider withdrawing funds. In general, this is not

recommended, but the severity of your situation may warrant a partial withdrawal. For now, simply record how much you have in retirement funds.

- **Do you have family or friends who can assist?** If you have relatives or friends who could help you through a rough patch, make a note of them and how much you think they could provide. Wait until you have fully assessed your situation and explored all your options before contacting them. That way, when you do call, you will know how much you need and for how long. Also, they will be far more likely to chip in if they feel confident that you are on top of the situation, realistic, and have a plan to turn it around.

- **Can you generate another source of income?** If the affected person can generate income in another manner, such as a temporary job or a sideline (such as selling items on eBay) note this and estimate the income. Also, if you have an older child, perhaps he or she could find part-time employment.

Please note that your first course of action should be to talk to your employer's human resources director, who will provide you with information pertinent to your situation and assist you in filing the necessary paperwork to apply for workers' compensation and COBRA, which will continue your health insurance. For more information about COBRA, check out Chapters 9 and 12.

What you need to do next is to create a detailed list that delineates your income and your expenses. All decisions will flow from determining your real income and your necessary expenses. Gather together the last six months' bills, bank statements, and paycheck stubs.

Calculating Your Income

Now that you have answered the questions in the preceding list, you should be able to realistically determine how much income you have for at least four to six months. Create a column that says "real income" and write down whatever unemployment insurance or disability insurance income you will receive, and then add the working partner's income. Please note that you want to use the take-home or net amount, not the gross amount. Often we think in terms of annual salary, but taxes and other deductions, such as health insurance payments, take a huge bite out of your salary and reduce your real income. The number of dependents that you claim affects the amount that is withheld for federal and state income tax from your paycheck. It's unlikely that changing your number of dependents will significantly alter take-home pay, but if it's fairly late in the year and you have covered what you can realistically determine will be your tax payment for that year, go ahead and reduce the number of dependents to increase your net pay.

Then, if you have sources of income you can verify from the preceding list, such as liquid assets or money contributed by relatives, add them to your income column. It is important to keep in mind that some of this income may not materialize. If it's iffy, don't assign it a real valuation in the income column. Instead, list these sources as "possible income" and rely solely upon your "real income" to create a workable plan.

Calculating Your Expenses

Now that you have a concrete idea of what's coming in each month, it's time to determine exactly what goes out the door monthly. Begin by making a list of all your ongoing monthly financial commitments and how much money each involves. In reviewing the list, make note of any places where you can immediately trim expenses. Again, the short-term versus long-term situation will greatly affect your decisions. If it's short-term, you may want—and be able—to float most of your expenses; if it's long-term, you may have no choice but to drastically cut, by selling the second car, relinquishing at least one cell phone, and cutting extraneous expenses, as well as reducing Internet, cable television, and clothing expenses.

Making Smart, Necessary, Immediate Decisions

Once you have worked your way steadily through this process, you'll have a list of necessary expenses and the exact amounts that you will need to generate to sustain them.

Now it's time to create a workable game plan to survive on one income. If your income will cover all your expenses, you're exceedingly lucky. Odds are, however, that you will be narrowly covered and will still need to trim expenses. Even if you are lucky enough to have unemployment income or disability income to sustain your family, you'd be wise to minimize expenses and save whatever money you can, just in case the situation drags on longer than expected.

If you are like the vast majority of families going from two incomes to one, your income will fall short of your needs. In this case, it's vital to first cover the most important bases—mortgage, food, utilities, and whatever is needed to sustain one income. If the situation will be long-term, you definitely may want to cash in liquid assets, call in family or friends, or even consider a consolidated loan. What we don't recommend, unless all else has failed, is an equity loan. You will have enough trouble covering one mortgage, and you don't want to risk losing your home by increasing your debt ratio. This is the equivalent of putting a Band-Aid on a ruptured appendix.

So, what you want to do is allocate your funds to the most important expenses and then pare down everything else as low as it can go. In this emergency stage, the most important tasks are to stay in your home, if possible, and to meet your family's primary needs. While you may be tempted, this is not the time to drop any insurance, nor to dip into your retirement funds—unless absolutely unavoidable. Hopefully, you'll be able to pay the essential bills and stay afloat until the situation improves. If you can cover everything except credit card and consumer debt, read on.

Negotiating Payments

If you are burdened with credit card or consumer debt, it will be essential to know exactly what you're facing. Take another clean sheet of paper, or a spreadsheet in Excel, to detail vital information for each credit card or loan, following the example provided:

	CREDIT CARD ASSESSMENT					
Creditor	Amount Owed	Minimum Payment	Interest Rate	Credit Limit	Due Date	What I Can Pay
Sears	$750	$39	16%	n/a	15th	$10
Bank of America	$6,200	$120	18.95%	$8,000	25th	$80
Macy's	$859	$45	24%	$900	16th	$15

Once you have your list, call each creditor personally. Rather than repeating your story, immediately ask for a supervisor who is able to make a decision concerning a suspension of interest and a reduced payment plan. Once you have that person on the line, tell her your situation—neither overdramatizing nor underplaying it—and ask what she can do to help. If you have been a solid customer for ten years, mention this as part of your negotiation. Tell the supervisor it's your intention to pay the debt in full and that you will offer steady payments in return for a suspension of interest and a reduced payment plan. If the supervisor won't cooperate, or won't offer what you need to stay afloat with this account, thank her anyway and proceed to the next creditor. Follow up the phone calls with a letter stating the terms the supervisor approved, and then adhere to the agreement.

If you find that the majority of your creditors will not cooperate, you may want to work with a consolidation service to negotiate on your behalf to zap the interest and lump all your credit card payments together. There are for-profit and not-for-profit agencies that will help you figure out what you can reasonably pay. Once you have settled on a program, the agency usually receives one lump monthly payment that they distribute to your creditors. It's not an ideal scenario, but if everything else has failed, it is better than reneging on payments.

If your situation is going to be long-term, and you have extra cash, you could also attempt to settle all your credit card debts. Often, a credit card company will accept as little as one-half of the total debt as payment in full, but you have to negotiate a deal and get it in writing before you pay. Keep in mind that doing so may affect your credit rating. You have to weigh the reality that slow payments or missed payments may affect it equally. Missed payments also may drive your interest rate up to a startling 24 percent. If you are in the throes of a long-term cutback, settling may be worth a drop in your rating to remove the debt and decrease your monthly net. Keep in mind, however, that the amount of debt forgiven could possibly be taxable unless you can prove that you were insolvent at the time. Please note that we cover credit card debt and how to dig out in depth in Chapter 5.

Staying Afloat

Now that you've figured how much money is coming in and how to maximize its distribution, it's time to put your plan into action. Be brave, bold, decisive, and consistent. Make the cuts you decided were necessary, and adhere to the budget. Even though you may feel deprived with some of the cutbacks, hopefully your situation will change for the better, and you'll be able to reward yourself for all the hard work. In the meantime, you'll learn valuable lessons about how to create and live within a budget, establishing discipline that will serve you well for the rest of your life. The most important task is to stay afloat and keep your family safe and well cared for until you can climb back up the ladder. It will be very important for you to stay on top of what's happening financially and to adjust your plan as needed. Never allow setbacks to get you down, and always make revisions as needed. That means no procrastinating!

Calculating Your Retirement Needs

Appendix B

WHETHER YOU'VE BEEN thrust into a one-income situation or are deciding whether you can electively choose to become a one-income household, knowing how much money you need to fund your retirement will be an important part of your budgeting decisions. This appendix has been designed to help you determine your retirement needs and assist you in making informed decisions.

Keep in mind that the amount you arrive at for your own required monthly savings is approximate. Notably, it's impossible to know what rate of return (after fees and taxes) you'll earn on your investments. It's a good idea to be conservative by saving an additional 5 or 10 percent on top of what you calculate as required monthly savings. You'll probably live for decades as a retiree, so you may as well over-reserve to ensure that you're able to live comfortably in your golden years.

The following steps will help you determine how much you should save each year so you can retire well.

1. Calculate your current annual personal living expenses. Your retirement expenses will exclude food and other expenses for your children, so exclude costs you can directly attribute to your children.
2. You can probably live on 75 to 90 percent of your current expenses in retirement—assuming that you reduce spending by not requiring expensive work clothing and decreasing transportation costs. Multiply your personal living expenses by 0.85 and divide by twelve to find your monthly retirement expenses.
3. Multiply the result of #2 by the inflation factor in the chart that follows, based on the number of years between now and the year you want to retire. The result is the amount of money you'll spend each month in retirement, after considering inflation:

INFLATION FACTOR

Years to retirement/Inflation factor

5	10	15	20	25	30	35	40	45	50
1.16	1.34	1.56	1.81	2.09	2.43	2.81	3.26	3.78	4.38

Assumes inflation is 3.0 percent per year

4. Estimate the number of years you'll live in retirement and the after-tax rate of return you'll earn on your investments during retirement. Then, using the following table, find the spending factor (the multiple of your first month's retirement spending that you'll need to have saved when you retire) that fits your parameters. Multiply the amount from #3 by this factor and write it down as you will need this number for Step 6. The result is the amount you should have in your portfolio when you retire.

SPENDING FACTOR

Years during retirement/After-tax rate of return earned during retirement

	5	10	15	20	25	30	35	40	45	50
4%	59	115	168	219	267	313	357	398	438	476
5%	58	110	157	200	238	274	306	335	362	386
6%	56	105	147	183	214	242	265	286	303	319
7%	55	100	167	168	194	215	232	246	258	268
8%	54	96	129	155	176	192	205	215	223	230
9%	53	92	122	144	161	173	183	190	195	199
10%	51	88	115	134	147	157	164	169	173	176
11%	50	85	108	125	136	143	149	152	155	157
12%	49	81	103	117	126	132	136	138	140	141

5. Multiply your total current savings by a future value factor from the following table, given the after-tax rate of return you expect on your investments before you retire, and the number of years between today's date and the date you want to retire. The result is the value of your current investments at the time you plan to retire:

FUTURE VALUE FACTOR

Years until retirement/After-tax rate of return before retirement

	5	10	15	20	25	30	35	40	45	50
4%	1.22	1.48	1.80	2.19	2.67	3.24	3.95	4.80	5.84	7.11
5%	1.28	1.63	2.08	2.65	3.39	4.32	5.52	7.04	8.99	11.47
6%	1.34	1.79	2.40	3.21	4.29	5.74	7.69	10.29	13.76	18.42
7%	1.40	1.97	2.76	3.87	5.43	7.61	10.68	14.97	21.00	29.46
8%	1.47	2.16	3.17	4.66	6.85	10.06	14.79	21.72	31.92	46.90
9%	1.54	2.37	3.64	5.60	8.62	13.27	20.41	31.41	48.33	74.36
10%	1.61	2.59	4.18	6.73	10.83	17.45	28.10	45.26	72.89	117.39
11%	1.69	2.84	4.78	8.06	13.59	22.89	38.57	65.00	109.53	184.56
12%	1.76	3.11	5.47	9.65	17.00	29.96	52.80	93.05	163.99	289.00

6. Subtract the result in #5 from the result of #4. This is the amount of savings you must accumulate beyond your current savings to meet your retirement savings goal.

7. Divide the result of #6 by the monthly savings factor in the following table, given the after-tax rate of return you expect on investments before you retire, and the number of years before you want to retire. The result is the amount you need to save every month to reach your retirement savings goal:

MONTHLY SAVINGS FACTOR									

Years until retirement/After-tax rate of return before retirement

	5	10	15	20	25	30	35	40	45	50
4%	65	145	243	361	505	680	893	1,153	1,468	1,852
5%	67	153	263	403	582	810	1,101	1,473	1,948	2,553
6%	68	161	285	451	672	969	1,366	1,897	2,608	3,560
7%	70	170	309	505	779	1,164	1,703	2,460	3,522	5,010
8%	72	179	336	566	905	1,403	2,134	3,209	4,788	7,108
9%	74	189	365	637	1,054	1,697	2,685	4,207	6,547	10,149
10%	76	199	397	716	1,230	2,058	3,391	5,538	8,996	14,565
11%	78	210	432	807	1,438	2,502	4,296	7,317	12,408	20,987
12%	80	221	471	910	1,685	3,050	5,455	9,695	17,166	30,333

EXAMPLE

Let's take time to do a sample calculation so that you can see how it works.

Step 1: Brenda is a 25-year-old single mother who figures that she spends about $2,500 per month on living expenses for herself, including rent, utilities, and so on. If Brenda owned her own home and expected to pay off the mortgage before she retired, she could exclude her mortgage payment from these monthly expenses. Brenda's annual personal living expenses total $30,000 ($2,500 × 12 = $30,000).

Step 2: She calculates the amount of income she would need in retirement each month if she retired today: $30,000 × 0.85 ÷ 12 = $2,125.

Step 3: Brenda wants to retire in forty years, when she's 65 years old. The relevant inflation factor is 3.26; thus, Brenda will spend $6,928 per month in retirement ($2,125 × 3.26 = $6,928.

Step 4: Brenda believes that she'll live to be 85 years old, but to err on the side of safety in her savings plan, she assumes that she'll live to be 90. She assumes that she will make 6 percent per year after tax on her investments during her twenty-five years of retirement. She finds the relevant savings factor is 214, and multiplies $6,928 by this factor. The result is $1,482,592, the amount Brenda will need in savings to be self-sufficient when she retires.

Step 5: Brenda has $15,000 invested in stocks and bonds; she assumes she'll earn an average of 8 percent per year after tax on her investments before retirement in forty years. She multiplies her $15,000 by the relevant future value factor, 21.72. The result, $325,800, is the expected value of her current investment portfolio the year she plans to retire.

Step 6: Brenda subtracts # 5 from # 4 to find the amount she needs to save on top of her current savings to fund retirement, $1,156,724.

Step 7: Brenda divides the result in #6 by the relevant monthly savings factor, 3,209. The result, $360.46, is the amount Brenda needs to invest every month until she retires to be able to fund her retirement expenses without any outside help.

What about Social Security?

Say you want to know how much you'll need to save for retirement assuming that you rely in part on Social Security payments. Repeat the exercise, reducing your annual required expenses (step #1) by the amount you expect to receive from social security after taxes. You can guesstimate the figure by looking up your estimated social security benefits at the Social Security Administration website (*www.ssa.gov*) and assuming that you'll receive perhaps 75 percent of that amount, net of taxes.

What about My Life Expectancy?

In a 2006 poll, the Society of Actuaries found that Americans chronically underestimate their life expectancy. Basing a financial plan on an underestimation of how long you'll live in retirement makes you more likely to outlive your savings. So while you don't want to massively oversave by assuming you'll live to be 120 years old, consider how old you might live to be, and then add five years to your lifespan just in case. You can find out what your life expectancy is by visiting the Centers for Disease Control and Prevention website (*www.cdc.gov*), where the information is found in the "Life Tables" put out by the National Center for Health Statistics. Most of us can expect to live to be 85 years old, but we hope you will have the resources to afford to live longer.

What about My Home Equity?

Another twist on the exercise: If you own your own home, despite the recent setbacks, and especially if you have several decades before retirement, you'll build up home equity over time that you can tap by selling or remortgaging the property. If you don't want to move, your home shouldn't be included in your investment portfolio, but, particularly the longer you own it pre-retirement, it will very likely become a valuable financial cushion, should you need to sell, in your old age.

What if I Want to Retire Early?

Repeat the preceding steps to figure out how much you need to save every month to retire at the desired age. If it's within your means, or something you can create, good for you!

Can I Rely on These Figures?

Again, please keep in mind that all the above calculations are approximate. If you're able to save what the exercise shows, you'll probably live well in retirement. However, if you save an extra 5 or 10 percent beyond the amount you calculate using the preceding tables, you'll live very well and thank yourself in retirement for being so wise. If, on the other hand, the retirement savings exercise shows that you need to save far more than you can afford every month to be able to retire well, now is the time to take corrective measures. By increasing savings and decreasing present-day spending, you can still build a se-cure future. If the worst that can happen is that you have to spend 15 percent less than you desired during retirement, you'll be in good company. In reality, most of us will have to cut back materially on spending at some point in retirement. The vast majority of us will have to humble ourselves and severely withdraw from America's culture of consumerism. There's nothing wrong with spending while you're young and reducing spending when you're old—again, you'll have lots of company—but when you're buying something nonessential, especially if it's a nonessential item that incurs bad debt (see Chapter 5 for an explanation of bad debt), it's both prudent and worthwhile to consider whether you'll have enough retirement income to cover important expenses, including housing, health care, transportation, clothing, food, and so on.

Once you have computed your needs, consult with an investment counselor to set realistic and achievable goals. Also keep in mind that you have to push the boundaries on what you think you can do, moni-tor your progress, and make smart investments that make your money grow without incurring excessive risk.

Resources

Appendix C

Credit Card Debt, FICO Scores, and Identity Theft • Consumer Loan Information (Including Home Equity Loan and Foreclosure Information) • Saving for College • Buying/Selling a Home or Car • Protecting Your Assets: Insurance • Taxes • Books about Women and Money • Books and Websites on Divorce and Remarriage • Resources for Frugal Living

Credit Card Debt, FICO Scores, and Identity Theft

CREDIT REPORTING BUREAUS

Equifax
P.O. Box 740241
Atlanta, GA 30374-0241
(800) 685-1111
www.equifax.com

Experian
P.O. Box 949
Allen, TX 75013-0949
(888) 397-3742
www.experian.com

TransUnion
P.O. Box 1000
Chester, PA 19022
(800) 916-8800
www.tuc.com

COUNSELING AND INFORMATION

National Foundation for Consumer Credit (NFCC)
Provides credit counseling.
(800) 388-2227
www.nfcc.org

National Association of Consumer Advocates (NACA)
A resource for finding a reputable law firm to handle credit disputes.
www.naca.net

Identity Theft Resource Center
Help with identity theft issues.
(858) 693-7935
www.idtheftcenter.org

Privacy Rights Clearinghouse
Help with identity theft issues.
(619) 298-3396
www.privacyrights.org

SEC Office of Investor Education and Assistance
450 Fifth Street NW
Washington, DC 20549-0213
(202) 942-7040
www.sec.gov

Federal Communications Commission
Consumer Information Bureau
445 12th Street SW
Washington, DC 20554
(888) CALL-FCC
www.fcc.gov

Social Security Fraud Hotline
P.O. Box 17768
Baltimore, MD 21235
(800) 269-0271
www.ssa.gov

BOOKS

Debt-Free by 30: Practical Advice for the Young, Broke, & Upwardly Mobile, by Jason Anthony and Karl Cluck.

Girl, Get Your Money Straight!: A Sister's Guide to Healing Your Bank Account and Funding Your Dreams in 7 Simple Steps, by Glinda Bridgforth.

Pay It Down: From Debt to Wealth on $10 a Day, by Jean Chatzky.

Your Credit Score: How to Fix, Improve, and Protect the 3-Digit Number That Shapes Your Financial Future, by Liz Pulliam Weston.

Consumer Loan Information (Including Home Equity Loan and Foreclosure Information)

Federal Reserve Consumer Help
P.O. Box 1200
Minneapolis, MN 55480
(888) 851-1920 (Phone)
(877) 766-8533 (TTY)
(877) 888-2520 (Fax)
E-mail: *ConsumerHelp@Federal Reserve.gov*
www.FederalReserveConsumerHelp.gov

FEDERALLY INSURED STATE NON-MEMBER BANKS AND SAVINGS BANKS

Federal Deposit Insurance Corporation
Consumer Response Center
2345 Grand Boulevard, Suite 100
Kansas City, MO 64108
(877) 275-3342
www.fdic.gov

NATIONAL BANKS AND NATIONAL BANK-OWNED MORTGAGE COMPANIES

Office of the Comptroller of the Currency
Customer Assistance Group
1301 McKinney Street
Suite 3450
Houston, TX 77010
(800) 613-6743
www.occ.treas.gov

FEDERALLY INSURED SAVINGS AND LOAN INSTITUTIONS AND FEDERALLY CHARTERED SAVINGS BANKS

Office of Thrift Supervision
Consumer Programs
6th Floor
1700 G Street NW
Washington, DC 20552
(800) 842-6929
www.ots.treas.gov

FEDERAL CREDIT UNIONS

National Credit Union Administration
Office of Public and Congressional Affairs
1775 Duke Street
Alexandria, VA 22314
(800) 755-1030
www.ncua.gov
For state-chartered credit unions, contact your state's regulatory agency.

OTHER GOVERNMENT INFORMATION SOURCES

Federal Trade Commission
Consumer Response Center #240
600 Pennsylvania Avenue NW
Washington, DC 20580
(877) FTC-HELP (382-4357)
www.ftc.gov

U.S. Department of Justice
950 Pennsylvania Avenue NW
Washington, DC 20530
(202) 514-3301
www.usdoj.gov/crt/housing/index.html

Federal Housing Finance Board
1777 F Street NW
Washington, DC 20006
(202) 408-2500
www.fhfb.gov

Department of Housing and Urban
Development
451 7th Street SW
Washington, DC 20410
(800) 669-9777
(800) 927-9275 (TTY)
www.hud.gov

Office of Federal Housing Enterprise
Oversight (OFHEO)
4th Floor
1700 G Street NW
Washington, DC 20552
(202) 414-6922
www.ofheo.gov

Saving for College

SEC's 529 Plan Website
www.sec.gov/investor/pubs/intro529.htm

Savingforcollege.com
Good information about 529 plans and
other means to save for college. Includes
side-by-side comparisons of state-spon-
sored 529 plans, which provide excellent
starting points for further research.
www.savingforcollege.com

The Federal Student Aid Websites
The definitive information about FAFSA
applications and federal education loans
are available on two websites. Either
website lets you sign up for a FAFSA
PIN (personal identification number)
and submit your FAFSA information
online.
http://studentaid.ed.gov
http://fafsa.ed.gov

You can also find more information
about all federal aid programs through
the U.S. Department of Education
brochure *Funding Education Beyond High
School* (published annually) via the following website:
*http://studentaid.ed.gov/students/publications/
student_guide/index.html*

U.S. Treasury
You can purchase up to $30,000 of each
kind of education savings bond each year
direct from the U.S. Treasury in denomi-
nations as low as $25.
http://treasurydirect.gov

Reputable Lenders

Two of the most well-known and reputable lending agencies are the Student Loan Marketing Association, more commonly known as Sallie Mae, and the nonprofit agency known as Nellie Mae:

http://salliemae.com
www.nelliemae.org

Buying/Selling a Home or Car

Bankrate.com

A good source for finding current average rates for money market funds, certificates of deposit (CDs), and checking accounts. The site also has a mortgage payment calculator that will show you how much your mortgage will cost per month, as well as how much of every payment is interest and how much pays down the principal balance of your loan.
www.bankrate.com

Edmunds.com

A good source for information about buying new and used cars; includes car reviews.
www.edmunds.com

Realtor.com

The National Association of Realtors Multiple Listing Service search engine allows you to search literally millions of homes for sale.
www.realtor.com

Yahoo!

This portal site's real estate page provides useful real estate information.
http://realestate.yahoo.com

Protecting Your Assets: Insurance

Life Insurance Calculators
www.choosetosave.org
www.tiaa-cref.org

Life Insurance Websites
www.term4sale.com
www.ameritasdirect.com
www.insure.com

Insurance Quotes
www.accuquote.com

Termquote
(800) 444-8376

Quotesmith
(800) 556-9393

Insurance Rating Companies
A.M. Best Company, Inc.
Ambest Road
Oldwick, NJ 08858
(908) 439-2200
www.ambest.com

Fitch Ratings
1 State Street Plaza
New York, NY 10004
(800) 75-FITCH
www.fitchibca.com

Moody's Investor Services
99 Church Street
New York, NY 10007
(212) 553-0300
www.moodys.com

Standard & Poor's Insurance Ratings
Services
55 Water Street
New York, NY 10004
(212) 438-2000
www2.standardandpoor.com

Weiss Research
15430 Endeavor Drive
Jupiter, FL 33478
(800) 289-9222
www.weissratings.com

Taxes

The Internal Revenue Service
You can find a ton of useful information
and download tax forms from the IRS
website. You can also call (800) 829-
1040 to speak to an IRS representative,
or go to your local IRS office (click on
"individuals" and then "contact my local
office" to find an office near you, and
keep in mind that June through February are the best months to go with a list
of questions).
www.irs.gov

Books about Women and Money

*The Everything® Guide to Personal Finance
for Single Mothers*, by Susan Reynolds and
Robert Bexton.

*Smart Women Finish Rich: Nine Steps to
Achieving Financial Security and Funding
Your Dreams*, by David Bach.

*Girl, Make Your Money Grow! A Sister's
Guide to Protecting Your Future and Enrich-
ing Your Life*, by Glinda Bridgforth and
Gail Perry-Mason.

*The Ten Commandments of Financial Hap-
piness: Feel Richer with What You've Got*,
by Jean Chatzky.

*Your Money or Your Life: Transforming Your
Relationship with Money and Achieving
Financial Independence*, by Joe Dominguez
and Vicki Robin.

*Making Bread: The Ultimate Financial
Guide for Women Who Need Dough*, by
Gail Harlow and Elizabeth Lewin.

*The Nine Steps to Financial Freedom: Prac-
tical and Spiritual Steps So You Can Stop
Worrying*, by Suze Orman.

*The Road to Wealth: Everything You Need
to Know in Good and Bad Times*, by Suze
Orman.

*Money, A Memoir: Women, Emotions, and
Cash*, by Liz Perle.

*The Soul of Money: Transforming Your Re-
lationship with Money and Life*, by Lynne
Twist.

Books and Websites on Divorce and Remarriage

BOOKS

Financial Custody: You, Your Money, and Divorce, by Joan Coullahan and Sue van der Linden.

Money Without Matrimony: The Unmarried Couple's Guide to Financial Security, by Sheryl Garrettand Debra A. Neiman.

WEBSITES

www.divorce-online.com
www.nolo.com

Resources for Frugal Living

BOOKS

The Everything® Meals on a Budget Cookbook, by Linda Larsen.

The Tightwad Gazette and *The Tightwad Gazette II*, by Amy Dacyczyn.

The Reader's Digest Penny Pincher's Almanac, by Don Earnest.

Frugal Living for Dummies: Practical Ideas to Help You Spend Less, Save More, and Live Well, by Deborah Taylor-Hough.

The Mom's Guide to Earning and Savings Thousands on the Internet, by Barb Webb with Maureen Heck.

WEBSITES

www.frugalliving.com
www.allthingsfrugal.com
www.thefrugalshopper.com
www.miserlymoms.com
www.lowermybills.com
www.mysimon.com
www.dealtime.com
www.ebay.com
www.ubid.com
www.priceline.com
www.travelocity.com
www.cheaptickets.com

Index

About the Author

Susan Reynolds is a freelance editor and author. She authored *The Everything® Guide to Personal Finance for Single Mothers* and *The 250 Personal Finance Questions for Single Mothers*, as well as five other nonfiction books. She currently is editing Adams Media's *Hero* series. After her divorce, Susan was drop-kicked into successful management of a one-income household. Learn more about Susan on *http:// Literarycottage.com*.

Lauren Bakken, CPA has been a public accounting and tax specialist for more than twelve years. In 2002, Lauren established her own business, Lauren Bakken CPA Inc., in Plymouth, Massachusetts. She provides personalized financial consultation and tax preparation services to individuals and small corporate businesses. Lauren also was divorced, and supported herself and her son by working full-time as an accountant while concurrently studying for and passing the CPA exam.